WE KILLED DARLAN

Algiers 1942

A Personal Account of the French Resistance in North Africa, 1940-1942

WE KILLED DARLAN

Algiers 1942

A Personal Account of the French Resistance in North Africa, 1940-1942

by Mario Faivre

Translated by Douglas W. Alden

Sunflower University Press®

1531 Yuma • P. O. Box 1009 • Manhattan, Kansas 66505-1009 USA

Nous avons tué Darlan
© Editions de la Table Ronde, France, 1975
English Language Edition © 1999 Sunflower University Press
Printed in the United States of America on acid-free paper.

Edited by Abigail T. Siddall

Layout by Lori L. Daniel

ISBN 0-89745-234-8

Sunflower University Press is a wholly-owned subsidiary
of the non-profit 501(c)3 Journal of the West, Inc.

Decree of 21 December 1945 by the Review Chamber of the Appeals Court of Algiers: Whereas, according to various letters in the dossier, particularly the final letter of F. Bonnier de la Chapelle written shortly before his execution, and according to documents discovered since the Liberation of France, it appears that Admiral Darlan was acting against the interests of France and that, therefore, the act that led to the sentencing of Bonnier de la Chapelle was in fact carried out in the interests of the liberation of France ... for these reasons, the judgment of the Permanent Tribunal of Algiers at the court martial of 25 December 1942, which sentenced Bonnier de la Chapelle to death, is annulled.

Contents

Mario Faivre at the time of the American landing in Algiers, November 1942.

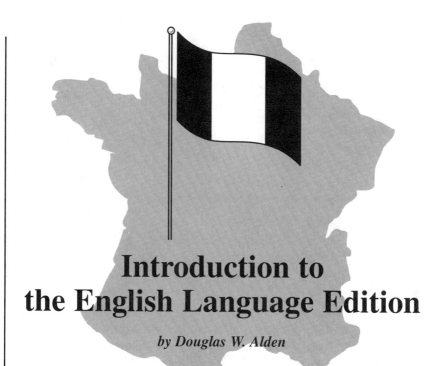

Introduction to
the English Language Edition

by Douglas W. Alden

O N THE SPRING OF 1944, after serving as an intelligence officer in the 8th Air Force, I was able to get myself reassigned to a more French-oriented activity with the Office of Strategic Services, the ancestor of the present Central Intelligence Agency. I was immediately sent as a briefing officer to Operation Sussex, whose mission was to parachute 120 young Free French officers into France to spy on the German army on and after D-Day.

Shortly after the war these former parachutists organized the Amicale du Plan Sussex — an association of veterans of Operation Sussex — with which, although I was anything but a war buff, I maintained cordial relations as we all grew older. Fifty years later I found myself more involved than ever, in commemorating the landings in Normandy, and my voice was heard on BBC radio talking about Operation Sussex. Captain Louis Guyomard, the perpetual president of the Amicale, sent me a small book recounting the experience of one of our parachutists in Alsace. He explained that he had just rediscovered this Mario Faivre, who had not joined the Amicale and whose real name he had not known because our men had to use false names even in training. I wrote to Mario, thanking him for his book, and he replied by sending me another book, one that he had published 25 years earlier, *Nous avons tué Darlan [We Killed Darlan]*.

This earlier book fascinated me, and I felt impelled to translate it. I knew very little about this other D-day, when American troops landed in North Africa in the first U.S. victory on land. How Darlan met his end was a matter of relative indifference to me. What attracted me so strongly was that this book was a dramatic day-by-day account (so spontaneous as to be somewhat unliterary and yet skillfully presenting setting and character) of the experiences of a young man, at first 18 and finally 20, who played a leading role in the incredible undertakings of the French Resistance at the time of the Allied landings. The role of the Resistance then was new to me, and because of my connections with the Resistance at a later date I was anxious that these exploits should be known.

Although I am a professor of French rather than of history, I have been forced to delve into history, since Mario's account raises a number of issues that will seem controversial to Americans. I have dealt with some of these issues in a Postscript. In this Introduction, I hope to present the setting for these events for readers as uninformed as I was when I first read Mario's book.

First, Algeria. When a powerful French army landed in Algeria in June 1830 and took the city of Algiers, the French had no intention of colonizing North Africa. The confrontation supposedly began with a slap in the face of the French consul by Hussein-Pascha, the last dey of Algiers, because of a complicated commercial transaction; but the real cause was far more serious. Although nominally still part of the Ottoman Empire, for centuries North Africa had been the lair of pirates, who dominated the local potentates. The situation was so grave that the government of Charles X of France decided to take action, but the decision probably cost the last Bourbon king his throne. On July 27, 1830, a revolution broke out in Paris. If Charles' army had been in Paris rather than in Algiers, he might have put down the revolt.

Replacing Charles X, the reluctant but more liberal Louis-Philippe, from the royal Orléans family, ascended the throne. The North African problem had not been solved. In 1832, Emir Abd-el-Kader was able to unify most of the Arabs and Berbers in a holy war, but the French finally began to increase their forces, and they captured the Arab leader in 1847. In 1881 the French expanded to the east, sending troops on the new railroad to Tunis and forcing the ruler there to accept a protectorate. In 1904, France forced a protectorate on the sultan of Morocco. (In 1925, a rebellion broke out in Morocco, known as the War of the Riff, in which two of Mario's characters, Henri Giraud and Alfred Pillafort, distinguished themselves.)

As early as 1834, the French began to refer to North Africa as "French possessions"; colonists from the entire Mediterranean area began to move in, and friendly Arabs joined the French army. Systematic colonization started in 1848 when the short-lived Second Republic settled thousands of paupers and political prisoners in Algeria. The Second Republic extended the new universal suffrage to French citizens in Algeria, making Algeria part of France with representation in parliament. Napoleon III was so interested in Arab culture that he began to grant citizenship to the natives, a procedure that was revoked after the Prussian defeat of France in 1870 because of pressure from colonists. In 1871, however, under the Crémieux decree mentioned by Mario, citizenship was granted to the Jewish population, which was as indigenous as the Arabs.

Mario grew up in a society as stable as that of France itself at the same period. He does allude to the PPA (Algerian Popular Party), but this seems to have been a negligible undercurrent of Arab resistance which would begin to have real importance only after 1950. Outside the Arab quarters, the cities were European, even to the street names borrowed mostly from Paris. The institutions were French, from the *lycées* and the university to the newspapers and literary circles. In 1934 the *colons*, the colonists, held one quarter of the arable land. Mario's family lived in a palatial villa surrounded by palm trees and flower beds and overlooking the city of Algiers; they had cars and a chauffeur, as well as large country estates. Because Mario had so many close Arab friends, one gets the impression that the Arabs had all been Frenchified, but the Arab world was nevertheless a separate one. The *colons* would not let it be otherwise. In spite of being second-class citizens, 185,000 natives fought for France in World War I. For World War II I have found only the statement that so many regiments were transferred from North Africa to metropolitan France that the colonies were practically defenseless; the bulk of these troops were surely native. A complicated procedure did exist for Arabs to become French citizens, but most did not take advantage of it, apparently because they were satisfied to live under Islamic law with their own courts and their own communal administrations. The French were only in the initial stages of founding a school system to bring Arabs and French together. In 1936, only 200,000 people had the right to vote in Algeria; the *colons* were obviously in control.

This life was destined to be overturned by events in Europe. On September 1, 1939, Hitler invaded Poland, and two days later France and England declared war. France thought it was ready for war but, relying on the underground fortresses of the Maginot Line in Alsace, it was not prepared for modern warfare with planes and tanks. On May 10, 1940, the Germans, repeating their strategy of World War I, attacked Belgium and simultaneously entered France at Sedan, and a few weeks later units of the Allied army, which had come to the aid of Belgium's King Leopold, were evacuated from Dunkirk. Colonel Charles de Gaulle, commanding the 4th armored division, had annihilated a German bridgehead on the Somme, taking 500 prisoners, but that little victory would make no difference.

For several years, with a book and articles critical of the military, de Gaulle had been arguing for a mobile army, with planes and tanks, and for replacing universal military service with a professional army. On June 6, Prime Minister Paul Reynaud called de Gaulle to Paris, promoted him to the temporary rank of brigadier general, and assigned him to the Ministry of Defense as undersecretary. On the 9th, Reynaud sent him to London to plead for the planes which England could no longer spare. Winston Churchill came over to Briare on the banks of the upper Loire to consult with Reynaud, and together they sent a desperate appeal to President Franklin Roosevelt (who did not immediately send the obvious answer: only Congress could declare war and the U.S. was still unprepared). On June 12, General Maxime Weygand, now the supreme French commander, ordered the army to retreat to a new line of defense along the Loire; two days later Paris was declared an open city. Reynaud summoned from Madrid the 84-year-old Marshal Philippe Pétain, the hero of Verdun, to be vice premier; and President Albert Lebrun, Reynaud, and the cabinet left Paris, eventually moving to Bordeaux. Many deputies and senators were also there; France was completely demoralized.

At this juncture, North Africa came back into the picture. De Gaulle persuaded Reynaud that the only solution was to transfer the government to North Africa in order to continue the fight. Admiral François Darlan, supreme commander of the navy, prepared orders for the French fleet to move to Britain or Martinique, or to scuttle itself if it was about to fall into German hands. General Bertrand Pujo was ready to send 500 planes to North Africa, and de Gaulle planned to send 780,000 troops. But none of this would happen, because Pétain insisted that he would stay in France to save the French people.

De Gaulle had been moving back and forth between London and Bordeaux, but on June 17 he left for London in a British plane with a pocketful of money given to him by Reynaud. His wife and children would escape by the last British ship out of Brest. Although a majority of the government and the deputies still expected to leave for North Africa, Reynaud resigned because of strong opposition from Pétain, Weygand, and their supporters, who were now determined to salvage what they could by requesting an armistice. President Lebrun, without parliamentary approval, appointed Pétain premier. Lebrun himself, still planning to leave, was browbeaten into submission by a Pétain supporter and finally stayed, soon to be eclipsed and forgotten. The *Massilia* was standing by in the Mediterranean, but only 26 members of parliament embarked for North Africa, where they ended up under arrest in Casablanca. On June 18, on the BBC, de Gaulle told the French that they had lost a battle but not the war; and on the 22nd, in the humiliating setting of the very railroad car at Rethondes, in the north of France, where the Germans had surrendered at the end of World War I, a French delegation signed the armistice.

Because Bordeaux was to be in the newly established Occupied Zone, whereas there was still a Free Zone in central and southern France, the French government moved first to Clermont-Ferrand and then to the watering place of Vichy, where there were many more hotels.

Now an event took place that Churchill, in his *Memoirs*, called a "Greek tragedy." In his hasty departure on the last British torpedo boat out of Bordeaux, Sir Ronald Campbell, the British ambassador, had received oral assurance that the mighty French fleet would never fall into the hands of the Germans. Of this fleet, four battleships and six destroyers were at Mers-el-Kébir, Morocco. On July 3, a powerful British fleet commanded by Admiral Sir James Somerville appeared offshore, mined the entrance to the harbor, and sent in an ultimatum. Admiral Marcel Gensoul had three choices: to join the British, to go to a British port from which the crews would be repatriated to France, or to send the ships with skeleton crews to Martinique, where they would be mothballed. Gensoul ordered his men to get up steam, to cheers from the seamen, who thought they were going to fight the Germans. He consulted the French admiralty but said only that the British wanted him to sink his ships. Next, he informed Somerville that he had secret orders from Darlan never to surrender to the Germans and that he was willing to cross the Atlantic but only with full crews. Somerville answered that he would fire unless Gensoul accepted one of the three original alternatives.

When Somerville eventually fired, the battleship *Strasbourg* and three destroyers managed to break out of the harbor and reach Toulon. The other ships were destroyed, with 1,297 French killed and 391 wounded. Overnight, Mers-el-Kébir turned the population of North Africa into mortal enemies of the British. It had the same effect on Darlan, who nevertheless remained resolved not to let the Germans get his fleet. The British bottled up another French fleet in Alexandria, Egypt, which was still under their control, and took over all French warships and merchant ships in British ports. The ships stationed at Algiers sailed just before the July 3 attack at Mers-el-Kébir, arriving safely at Toulon a day later.

One surprising provision of the armistice was that the French could keep their fleet if it was mothballed. The procedure had already begun at Mers-el-Kébir, rendering the fleet unable to defend itself effectively. The French were also allowed an army of 100,000 men, and at the time of the Allied landings in November 1942, there was one army in the Free Zone and a second army, of 110,000, in North Africa. The Germans had even liberated French officers like General Alphonse Juin, because they had North African expertise. The Germans obviously believed that the French would defend North Africa against non-Germans.

Allowing the French government to exist was a major concession, since other countries like Belgium and Holland were all under German gauleiters. The reason was that Hitler intended to invade England next, so that a peaceful and cooperative France would be an asset and would require fewer troops if not fully occupied. Marshal Pétain was convinced that Hitler would be in London in a short time and that the only way he could save France was to appease him.

Pétain, having become a father figure who would save the average Frenchman, inaugurated a "family values" program that soon expanded into a propaganda campaign like those of the reigning dictators, with

Pétain's picture posted everywhere. Every time Pétain appeared in a town, he was greeted by a little girl bearing flowers. Inspired perhaps by the American Civilian Conservation Corps, as one American historian has said, but more likely by the Hitler Jugend, Pétain's program included the Chantiers de la Jeunesse, designed to produce healthy and productive youth. Since this compulsory program had a military component, it not only replaced universal military service but also, though without arms, would supply the manpower for an army if the time ever came. After the assassination of Darlan, Mario was a noncom in a unit of the Chantiers that became a tank regiment. Earlier, he was in the naval equivalent of the Chantiers, the Eclaireurs Marins (Sea Scouts), which had sent him to a naval officer training school.

Pétain did not believe in democracy and blamed the Third Republic for the French defeat, an opinion which so many seemed to share at the time that the Third Republic, represented by its president, chamber of deputies, and senate, meeting in Vichy, voted itself out of existence and conferred on Pétain the title of chief of state, with the power to govern by decree. Pétain never acted like a dictator in the style of Hitler or Mussolini but, as a military officer, he expected to give orders and to be obeyed without argument. That did not prevent others from attempting to influence his decisions, but he never accepted the advice of General Weygand, who was now urging him to move his administration to North Africa. The Germans, who seemed to know almost everything that was going on in the innermost French circles, insisted that Weygand be removed from the government; Pétain responded by sending him to take charge in North Africa. What was left of the French officer corps in the Free Zone continued to make plans to fight the Germans if the time came, but Pétain was not plotting resistance: his whole strategy was to keep the Germans satisfied and to get as many concessions from them as possible. Although he had never joined royalist or fascist parties, his sympathies had always been rightist. The abrogation of the "Rights of Man" guaranteed by the French constitution was one of Pétain's dictatorial decrees, and a second measure, growing out of the anti-Semitism of the Right, was to curtail the rights of Jews in the Free Zone and later to deliver to the Nazis all foreign Jews living there.

Surprisingly, although he despised him, Pétain kept in his cabinet as Foreign Affairs minister a former premier, once a moderate but now a rightist, Pierre Laval. During the summer of 1940, with British support and that of the governor of Tchad, de Gaulle's Free French were gaining territory in Central Africa, and Laval urged Pétain to declare war on Britain. Instead, Pétain sent an inconspicuous philosophy professor, Louis Rougier, on a secret mission to assure Churchill that France would never make war on Britain.

By autumn, relations between Pétain and Laval had turned sour. Cabinet members advised Pétain to force Laval to resign because he was spending too much time in Paris with the Germans. When Laval was in Vichy trying to persuade the marshal to attend a ceremony in Paris for the return of the ashes of Napoleon's son (a gesture thought up by Hitler with the help of a French collaborator), Pétain suddenly ordered his entire cabinet to resign and placed Laval under house arrest. Now Pétain created the new position of "head of government" and called in a liberal former premier, Pierre-Etienne Flandin. The Germans exerted such pressure for Laval to be recalled that Pétain yielded to the extent of offering him a minor cabinet post, which he refused.

Since the Germans did not like Flandin, Pétain was forced to replace him with Admiral Darlan. Darlan was respected by his navy, but the public already had a low opinion of him, and later he aroused the hostility of the army by lowering the retirement age and dismissing many generals. He also made all of the military swear allegiance to Pétain. He was very vain, often traveling with a navy band, and he kept a special train which, because of its priorities, upset the normal schedules. But he was a very efficient administrator and surrounded himself with technocrats and a surprising number of outstanding humanists and educators. The new American ambassador, Admiral William D. Leahy, appointed in the hope that admirals would have something in common, referred to him as "Popeye." Initially, like Pétain, Darlan thought the Germans to be invincible, even when they failed to overrun England, and that the only realistic policy was collaboration.

In the Occupied Zone, the Germans were executing hostages in retribution for isolated attacks, pillaging French resources, and forcing Frenchmen to work in German factories. In June 1941 they attacked Russia. German troops were in Greece and Libya, where they had had to reinforce the incompetent Italians. General Erwin Rommel's army was within 80 kilometers of Alexandria. Then the Japanese, on December 7, sank the American fleet at Pearl Harbor, and the picture changed.

In early 1942 Darlan reversed policy and openly opposed new German pressures on France. The result was that the Germans forced Pétain to replace him with Laval, although Darlan was still commander of the French armed forces. In his speeches Laval was still maintaining that France should enter the war on the German side. By this time Pétain, who had already seemed to be a tired old man when Admiral Leahy first met him, was making few decisions. The Gestapo had been brought into the Occupied Zone and, in the Free Zone, Joseph Darnand's Service d'Ordre de la Légion burned the synagogue at Nice.

On April 17, using a rope 45 meters long made by a fellow prisoner, General of the Army Henri Giraud, aged 63, slid down the wall of the fortress of Königstein and took a train for Switzerland. The Germans wanted him back, but he was given free rein in the Free Zone, and, after swearing allegiance to Pétain, he contacted every available French general, including Weygand, now in retirement, to prepare for what he hoped would be an American landing in southern France. He wanted Weygand to lead, but the former commander in North Africa refused, alleging that he was too old.

Things were going badly for the Axis. Hitler's army was going down in defeat at Stalingrad. In Libya, Rommel was retreating before the British army of General Bernard Montgomery. When Laval answered Hitler's summons to come to Berchtesgaden, he took a cyanide pill with him.

General de Gaulle, in London, had not been allowed by Churchill to form a government in exile like those of the Belgians, Dutch, Poles, and Norwegians, because the French already in London, or arriving there on their way to exile in the United States, would not support him. De Gaulle got no help from the intellectuals, who largely opposed him, as did a majority of the 9,000 French refugees in the United States. Churchill told de Gaulle that all he could do for him was to make him the commander of a French army of volunteers fighting alongside the English. Some 900 soldiers of the Foreign Legion, who had been on an aborted expedition to Norway in support of Finland, signed up with de Gaulle, while retired Admiral Emile Muselier organized with great skill a Free French navy and an air force. When the Central African colonies of Tchad, Cameroun, French Congo, and Gabon more or less spontaneously threw out the Vichy authorities, de Gaulle set up a capital in Brazzaville and arranged for lend-lease and a powerful radio station from the United States, becoming thus a head of state, although at this time he was not recognized as such by any government. At the same time he maintained his original head-quarters in London.

At Brazzaville de Gaulle began his decrees with, "We, General de Gaulle," just as though he were the king of France, said the British. Not being accustomed to an independent de Gaulle, Churchill became more and more annoyed and at one point threatened to cease all financial and logistical support for the otherwise penniless Free French. Like Pétain, de Gaulle had one objective, to save France and its Empire, and he intended to do it in his own way. A career officer, he was accustomed to giving orders and seeing them obeyed.

In July of 1940, de Gaulle had created his own intelligence organiza-tion, the Bureau Central de Renseignement et Action, commanded by André Dewavrin, alias Colonel Passy. At this time resistance in France was mostly intellectual, consisting of clandestine tracts and newspapers like *Combat* that were passed around. On October 23, after two German officers had been shot at Nantes and Bordeaux, bringing about the execu-tion of 48 French hostages, de Gaulle condemned random shooting in a BBC broadcast. A few days later, Jean Moulin, a former prefect who had been dismissed for opposing the Germans at Chartres, arrived in London via Lisbon and persuaded de Gaulle to contact the principal Resistance networks that were springing up spontaneously in France and unite them in a "secret army." In January 1941, Moulin parachuted into the Free Zone with two assistants, and over the next months he brought together the three major Resistance organizations of the Free Zone, one of them led by Emmanuel d'Astier de la Vigerie, the brother of one of Mario's heroes. These groups pledged allegiance to de Gaulle. This was not yet unani-mity; it was only after the assassination of Darlan in November 1942 that Moulin assembled at a clandestine meeting the leaders of the Resistance in both zones and representatives from all major parties of the Third Republic, including the communists, and persuaded them to support de Gaulle. Captured by the Germans, Moulin died after torture in August 1943.

Without a trace of sentimentality, Roosevelt maintained relations with Vichy to keep an eye on things and to influence the government. In the latter respect, he failed. Ambassador William C. Bullitt had beaten a hasty retreat from Bordeaux, and it was Robert D. Murphy, counselor at the Paris embassy, who became *chargé d'affaires* at Vichy. In October 1940, long before Pearl Harbor, Roosevelt summoned Murphy to Washington and, with a map of North Africa spread on his desk, discoursed on the strategic importance of the region and the possibility of establishing a useful relationship with Weygand, in charge at that time. Murphy was dispatched to North Africa as the president's representative, and soon afterward Lieutenant Colonel Robert A. Solborg of Army Intelligence, using as cover his normal role as an international businessman, went to North Africa to contact, if possible, dissident elements. At Casablanca he found some young officers, led by Captain André Beaufre, who were already plotting future resistance and who would be pleased to receive American arms. Solborg submitted their requests to Washington but received no reply. At this juncture the whole conspiracy was discovered by Inspector André Achiary, head of Vichy counterintelligence, who later, as a loyal friend of Mario, continued to fulfill his official duties while participating in the Resistance. Achiary did his best to cover up and protect the conspirators; he had to take Beaufre and Major Léon Faye into custody, but they got light sentences, being simply ordered out of North Africa and back to the Free Zone. Beaufre later came back clandestinely to North Africa.

Beaufre had made the acquaintance of Jacques Lemaigre-Dubreuil, a wealthy industrialist, owner of vegetable oil factories in North Africa, who could move freely between Vichy France and North Africa. He was a personal friend of Laval and a rightist, but he also hated the Germans and probably hoped to play a major role in any government after the war. Eventually he became one of the "Group of Five" leading the Resistance in North Africa, and the contact who shuttled back and forth between Giraud and the other leaders. When Achiary called in Lemaigre-Dubreuil for questioning, each discovered what the other was doing. Soon Lemaigre-Dubreuil brought from Vichy Jean Rigault, editor of the newspaper *Le Jour,* which the industrialist owned. Rigault, authoritarian by persuasion, was to become another of the Group of Five. Meanwhile in Oran another group of young officers had founded a Resistance movement which included Lieutenant Henri d'Astier de la Vigerie, a future member of the Group of Five. Member of a noble family, he was a royalist at heart, and most historians call him a Gaullist because he kept in touch with his brother Emmanuel. Mario presents him as strongly opposed to de Gaulle. The fourth member of the group was Colonel Jean Van Hecke, commander of the Chantiers de la Jeunesse for North Africa. Van Hecke had d'Astier transferred to the Chantiers so that the latter might be able to move freely throughout North Africa for the business of the Resistance. The fifth member was the diplomat Jacques Tarbé de Saint-Hardouin, about whom Mario knew little. The Group of Five began to function as a unit starting in January 1942.

A few days after Pearl Harbor, Churchill and Roosevelt discussed plans for an invasion of North Africa, but they were soon dropped in favor of an attack on the Continent across the English Channel. At the end of May 1942, the Soviet Foreign Minister Molotov told Roosevelt that the Russian situation was becoming so desperate that his country might make peace with the Germans, and that the only way out was for the Allies to open up a second front. Immediately, without consulting Churchill, Roosevelt began to plan Operation Torch, the invasion of North Africa. Churchill approved Torch after the failure of an attack on Dieppe in August, and it became a joint operation. Sensing that something was in the wind, de Gaulle asked to meet with General George C. Marshall and General Dwight D. Eisenhower in London. He explained at length the capabilities of the Free French forces, but the complete silence of the Americans convinced him that he was wasting his time and he abruptly left the room.

Meanwhile the Group of Five was at work. Lemaigre-Dubreuil had made contact with General Giraud and had persuaded him to take part in an invasion of North Africa. Giraud designated General Charles Mast, the new chief of staff of the XIXth army corps in Algeria, as his representative. Mast had been a prisoner at Königstein, but he had been released to serve as the Vichy military attaché in Tokyo. Ready to play a primary role in the Resistance, Mast contacted Murphy, who was impressed by him, and he urged Murphy to accept Giraud as the French leader. At this juncture, Colonel Solborg, now a secret agent of the newly created OSS under command of "Wild Bill" Donovan, instead of going to a meeting with Donovan, went hastily to North Africa without orders. Thinking that he had more authority than he really had, Murphy let him deal with the Resistance leaders, who on June 15 drew up a document for Washington which insisted on the need for a military conference, on an economic agreement similar to the one earlier accorded Weygand, and that the governmental authority be given to the French (including a guarantee of the integrity of the French Empire). Solborg took the document to Washington; Donovan refused to read it and fired Solborg for disobeying orders.

On September 17 Murphy was called to Washington for consultation; he did not return to North Africa until October 4. D-day in North Africa had been set for November 8. During the short time remaining, Murphy conferred with the Group of Five, revising the rejected June 15 document. This new document was to be the source of numerous misunderstandings on both sides.

Heeding the recommendation that there be a military conference between the Resistance leaders and the Americans, General Eisenhower sent to that meeting none other than the general who was to command the entire operation, Mark W. Clark. The secret rendezvous was to be in the villa of a *colon* near Cherchell, on the Algerian coast. In his memoirs, *Calculated Risk,* General Clark describes this "adventure." With several other American officers, Clark embarked at Gibraltar on the somewhat obsolete *Seraph,* a British submarine passing for American (because of the Mers-el-Kébir incident). A slow journey on the surface and sometimes under water brought them finally to Cherchell in the early hours of October 21. Before they could disembark, the arrival of some local fishing boats obliged them to go back out to sea and submerge. The next day before daybreak they landed from their collapsible boats and were met by Murphy and his assistant, Ridgway Knight, accompanied by some of the French delegation. General Mast arrived with several officers, some of whom stood guard outside while the deliberations were going on in the morning. Mast left after lunch, which was served by the owner himself, as he had sent his servants away. Suddenly they were warned that the police were coming. Some of the French drove off quickly, while Clark and his officers hid under the floor in the wine cellar. Murphy and Knight pretended to be guests at a wild party. The police had been alerted by the servants, who had become suspicious when they were sent away.

After the police left, the American officers hid in the woods until dusk. As they were trying to get into their collapsible boats in a stormy sea, Clark lost his trousers, which he had already taken off because they were weighted down by the gold brought along for an escape if necessary. The next day they sent a Frenchman to hire a fishing boat, but the suspicious fisherman refused to sail. Clark, shivering and barefoot, went back to the house for clothes, but the police returned, and Clark jumped down from a 10-foot wall and disappeared into the woods. The group finally managed to get back through a still-rough sea to the submarine and were eventually picked up by flying boats from Gibraltar.

I have told this amusing story in some detail because Mario seemed to know nothing about it, or omitted it because of the seriousness of the meeting, which in his version might have lasted a full day, at least. It was a serious meeting for Clark, as well, but in a totally different way. He wanted strategic information on the fortifications along the coast; Mast brought it. He wanted confirmation that the French army would not oppose the Americans because they would obey a general named Giraud, whom Murphy had recommended in a cable. He half expected that Giraud would be at the meeting, but he learned that an "American" submarine would have to go and get him. Mast, who inspired confidence, assured Clark that he could count on Giraud. Clark does not mention that Mast had with him Colonel Louis Jousse and Navy Commander Barjot, who figure in Mario's narrative, nor does he seem to know that the Group of Five was well represented: Van Hecke, Rigault, d'Astier de la Vigerie assisted by Bernard Karsenty. What counted most for Mario was what he called the Clark-Giraud protocol, the document that Murphy brought to the meeting. Clark says nothing about this, nor does he mention that other point so crucial to Mario: the plan for the Resistance to immobilize the French army in Algiers.

Now we turn to Mario's account, to me more interesting than these controversial matters. I have changed his misspellings of certain names and clarified, within the text, a few expressions or historical discrepancies. Otherwise, this is Mario's story as he recorded it in 1975.

Preface

by Jean-Bernard d'Astier de la Vigerie

$\mathcal{I}$T WAS IN 1941, in Algiers, that I met Mario. We were the same age and held the same opinions, and we quickly formed a solid friendship that has continued undiminished since that time.

We used to meet frequently at the home of his parents at Mont-Hydra. Mario, who during a life largely devoted to action has remained an accomplished musician, would play the piano — the "Pathétique Sonata," which held so much meaning during that period — while night fell in the gardens above the town. Leaving the lights off, we would prolong the brief African dusk.

Mario was more mature than I, and at 18 he had already seen action. I had heard of his duel with one of his friends on Christmas Day and his attempt to reach England, which had mobilized all the security forces in the Oujda region. Next followed his very important role in the preparation for the Allied landing of November 8, 1942. I should mention in passing that Mario has not read any of the many publications about the subject, although they frequently mention him. After an outstanding career in the parachute forces, where he

accumulated citations, he devoted himself to the Algerian question from
the end of hostilities until the final days of French Algeria [1958].

I did not take part in the landing. Having enlisted in 1939, after the
defeat I came back to North Africa, where I was put into the Chantiers de
la Jeunesse and posted some distance from Algiers. After the landing, on
my return to Algiers I divided my time between Abbé Cordier and Mario.
We were at the heart of the monarchist plot, which met with approval from
everyone, including republicans. Then came the murder of Darlan, in
which Mario and I acted alongside Bonnier, our friend. This is the account
of those events. For a long time I have urged Mario to publish it, to reveal
finally the truth of that affair. The accounts that have appeared — and they
are many — have hardly touched it.

Abbé Cordier has been gone from us since November 1973. Out of
respect for this man of deep faith, and concerned with protecting matters
that the actors in this drama considered state secrets whose disclosure
might harm more important state interests, Mario had no intention of
telling this story. We have encouraged him to do so.

I affirm that the account of the Darlan episode that you are going to read
is scrupulously exact in all details, whether of actions or of words or of
reported conversations. I am grateful to Mario for having written it especially as a memoir to our Abbé Cordier, about whom have appeared many
statements both injurious and false.

Thank you, my dear Mario: here we have a moment of history indis-
putably and definitively established, written (to your credit) in the spirit of
the sentiments we were experiencing at the time, without the interference
of those we might feel now, after all that has happened.

Jean-Bernard d'Astier de la Vigerie [1975]

Prologue

O N THAT EARLY AFTERNOON OF MARCH 6, 1941, we watched the countryside west of Oran roll by outside the windows of the train. After a long stop we had just left Sainte-Barbe-du-Trélat, where our cars had been shunted onto a siding at some distance from the station to change locomotives. As the train had started moving again, we had noticed, without paying much attention, some Algerian infantrymen and civilians running up and surrounding the station. They were blowing whistles and shouting.

The idea had not even entered our minds that all this commotion was because of us.

As far as the eye could see, in tight rows covering the ochre-colored soil right up to the tawny hills where the Atlas Mountains began, grapevines were ready to burst into bloom. Abruptly we would move into the restful shade of an orange grove bordered with somber cypress trees, or through the pink and white splendor of orchards in flower. From time to time we could see the buildings of a farm, plain structures without charm, the houses of pioneers.

Sometimes we sensed a profound tranquillity as we passed through a eucalyptus wood or a plantation of olive trees where oleanders grew. Under the
clear blue sky the limpid, gentle light aroused in us a sensation of warm,
almost physical, alliance with this uncomplicated natural scene. Seated on
the wooden benches of our old, undivided, third-class car, we exchanged
quiet remarks. The adventure pleased us.

Almost all of the passengers in the car were Moslems, squeezed together on the seats, sitting on the floor of the central corridor, or standing in
the midst of baskets, bundles, strings of garlic, trussed-up chickens.
Around us were the gray or brown Arab robes, the khaki uniforms of the
Algerian infantrymen, bright splashes of color from the green or pink
shawls of the Moorish women.

We were sitting opposite each other. Beside me was Mohamed Sayah,
a young Moslem of 19 from a prominent family of the Orléansville region.
Opposite me was my good friend Roger Rosfelder, who had just turned 18,
next to René Guéraud, 19. I was a few months older than Roger.

After a while we talked less because of the noise of the train and the
conversations and discussions going on around us. From time to time we
exchanged a glance of complicity as we passed our straw-covered water
bottle around. Since leaving Algiers at four in the morning we had already
snacked two or three times on the food in Roger's scout knapsack: bread
bought at the stop at Orléansville, sausage, smoked ham, some oranges.

The train was supposed to arrive at Tlemcen at eleven o'clock that
evening. We no longer thought about our plans because they were so
sketchy and subject to so many different variations. We would get off the
train at Tlemcen, where thanks to Sayah we would be lodged in a discreet
Moslem home. Once there, we were to contact someone who would
arrange for *passeurs,* guides, to take us across the mountains of the Moroccan frontier. In spite of the many risks, it was the best way for us to
reach the English naval base at Gibraltar, then move on to London, where
we planned to enlist in the Free French forces.

Sidi-bel-Abbès. In front of the buildings of the station, especially
around the passenger exit, we could see infantry posted. The stop seemed
to last a long time.

Suddenly the passengers standing between the seats were violently
pushed aside by several Europeans who rushed toward us. Not toward us,
toward Roger.

"You are Roger Rosfelder?"

They threw themselves on him, pinned his arms down, even though he was still seated. There were four of them. One shouted,"That's the one, Chief, sort of fat, with a round head, light eyes. We got a good look at him from below!"

Another one demanded, "Show me your papers!"

We didn't have any false identity papers. Roger said, "That's my name."

"You are under arrest. Come with us." Two or three of them seized him and began to drag him off.

"What about my things?" asked Roger.

"Where?"

"The knapsack."

They snatched it up. I held out the water bottle, and one of the men took it. The passengers had moved aside, opening a passageway, and the policemen got off the train with Roger. Everyone in the car had become silent. Two minutes later we heard the conductor's whistle, and the train got under way.

Night fell, and in the car the electric lights came on, as we rolled on toward the west. Since the departure from Sidi-bel-Abbès we had not exchanged a word. None of us thought of giving up, but Roger's departure had left a void.

We had not expected to be pursued before we crossed the Moroccan frontier disguised as Arabs. Clearly the police were only after Roger, and therefore the leak must have concerned him alone. His younger brother, André, was supposed to cover up for him. Very clever and trustworthy, although he was only 15, he was to mislead people at the *lycée* to explain Roger's absence and then produce Roger's letter to his parents only on the third day. What had happened?

Since the leak concerned only Roger, our chances of succeeding were still good. Guéraud was sure that his parents had kept quiet. Sayah had no reason to be anxious, because he had told his parents that he was taking a trip with friends. For my part, my parents surely did not give the alert. Once before, last October, I had disappeared for a few days, leaving a message to inform them of my intentions: "I will come back if it doesn't work." I wasn't even able to leave Algiers that time. I went back home, and they told no one. Theoretically we could still succeed. We knew that Roger would say nothing.

We were coming to the village of Lamoricière, the last stop before Tlemcen. From time to time a furtive glance from one or another of the passengers turned toward us, but it carried no hostility, and no one asked any questions.

Emerging out of the darkness, our train stopped beside the dimly lighted platform. We could barely see the buildings, but the Algerian infantrymen were there with fixed bayonets. Gendarmes were guarding the exit with a few men in civilian clothes. We did not budge, and a few minutes later the train started up.

"There were not enough of them; they were afraid to come and get us," guessed Sayah.

We no longer had any doubt: there was a whole military force out to catch us, and at Tlemcen, the terminus of the line, there would be people waiting for us. Jump off while the train was moving? In the darkness of this moonless night, you couldn't even see the embankment; moreover, in this half-deserted countryside we would have been quickly spotted.

"If I'd known, I would not have asked you to come with us," I told Sayah.

He looked at me, his face eager. "Mario, I'm your pal, aren't I?"

Guéraud remained silent. Things were not happening the way we had thought.

More noticeable than the noise of the train, a silence settled inside the car. There were fewer people, no Europeans; a few seats were empty. Perhaps some worried passengers had moved into other cars. Some were eating cakes, others beans, and everyone maintained a discreet silence. An elderly Moorish woman came over to offer us some rye bread, and we accepted. The Algerian infantrymen in the car, all Moslems, who had impassively witnessed Roger's arrest, sat down on a bench beside us. One of them, a noncom with a big mustache, offered me a piece of chicken.

"Eat, you must eat."

I took the chicken, and the others, too, gave us the best part of their meals.

"You'll need it. At Tlemcen they're going to arrest you. You must keep up your strength."

No one asked any questions. I told them, "We want to fight the Boche."

They nodded. "That's perfectly normal," responded the noncom.

We felt better. Our weariness and the need for secrecy weighed less heavily now, and we needed to prepare for our arrival. There was no question of turning our railroad car into a fortress: that would be utterly stupid. We entrusted our two automatic pistols, our bullet clips, our bullets, to the infantrymen. If we could get out of the station, they would give them back to us; otherwise they would keep them. All of that took place quickly under the eyes of all of the passengers, but we knew that no one would give us away. If we were arrested, we would just say that we wanted to see the countryside. A banal escapade. We would get off the train very naturally, all three of us together, like people who had nothing to hide. We would keep the whole episode simple so that we could be set free as soon as possible.

In the black night the train headed down the slope into Tlemcen, until suddenly we were under the lights of the station. It was in a state of siege; there was a cordon of soldiers with rifles in hand and gendarmes armed with carbines.

The passengers began to get off. Our military friends went first so that no one would see us together; then we walked toward the exit.

Standing idiotically at attention, members of a Vichy organization, the Legion of Combatants, their berets pulled down to one side, their eyes expressionless, their chins high in the air, had come in large numbers to affirm their allegiance to the regime and to participate morally in our arrest.

We passed between some gendarmes and approached the narrow neck of the exit, where several policemen in civilian clothes were waiting for us. There we had to proceed one by one. The first policeman did not react, nor did the second. Suddenly I had a hope that all this did not concern us, and I could see myself going through the building without difficulty, in company with Sayah and Guéraud. But then things happened quickly.

"You have your papers?"

"Yes."

"Your name is Faivre?"

"Yes."

I was seized, carried off, dragged away by a multitude of hands, and I found myself in a room in the station. A police officer rushed in: "Where are the others?"

He showered me with blows, preventing me from answering even if I had wanted to. In the midst of it I saw Guéraud come in, held by two policemen, and Mohamed Sayah, who cried, "Me, too, I'm with them!"

They insulted us: "Bastards, swine!" We were thrown into automobiles, and a few moments later we got out at the headquarters of the Mobile

Guard, where the superintendent began to interrogate me. Sayah and Guéraud were under guard in a nearby room. Two inspectors held me, twisting my arms behind my back.

The superintendent's name was Faux. He spread out the contents of my billfold on the desk. A few papers, some money. He looked at my sea scout card.

"This turd has the audacity to be a sea scout!"

Then he started to bellow: "We know everything about you, but I want to hear you admit it. So, where were you going?"

"Well, we saw some posters, 'Visit picturesque Tlemcen,' so we came here."

His already crimson face turned the color of an eggplant, and he rushed forward to strike me. I tried to kick him with all of my strength, but the policemen pulled me violently backwards. He roared, "Put him in jail! In jail with the melons!" [a slang word for Arabs].

The men dragged me into a hallway, opened a little door, and pushed me in. After almost falling down two or three steps, I found myself in complete darkness. The cell was a kind of stinking cesspool with a slimy floor. I took off my raincoat (it belonged to my father), stretched it out on the floor, and sat on it.

What was going to happen now? Would we be tried, or sent directly to the concentration camp of Boghar on the stony high plateau of the southern Algerian Atlas Mountains, where those who refused to accept the fall of France were shut up behind barbed wire? All this display of force to capture us! I couldn't help smiling. How inept it was!

In the train, the noncom had said, "That's perfectly normal." That had given me particular pleasure because it was the same answer I had given my father after a first attempt to escape. It hurt him to know that I wanted to fight. As a liberal writer he had spent his entire life in a combat for peace. For him, the only possible struggle was an intellectual one, but nevertheless I remembered that in one of his editorials shortly after Munich he concluded that Hitler had to be killed to avoid a worldwide massacre. In September 1939 he had given up his crusade for peace. "Now," he said, "it would be helping the other side." We had not returned to Paris.

I had witnessed the early months of 1940 almost as a stranger. Nothing was happening. An intensive propaganda campaign told us every day that Hitler had lost the game, that Germany was at the end of its resources and was going to be forced to lay down its arms without ever fighting. A slogan, posted everywhere, asserted, "We will win because we are the stronger." I was working hard, especially on music, and was calmly waiting to be called up. Then came May and June. In a few days the German armies, well trained, well equipped, well supplied with intelligence, isolated and then destroyed the French forces and invaded most of metropolitan France. So I saw the ruin of my hopes — a life that I had desired for years — and I perceived that, whether I wanted it or not, the war was now my concern.

Algiers, whose radio from one hour to the next announced ever more disastrous news, was in a state of agitation. Everyone was thinking, "Paris is occupied, now Algiers is the capital." No one imagined that the struggle could end because France had been invaded. The fleet in the harbor was a symbol, a guarantee that the Empire was intact. The aviators who succeeded in landing at the Maison Blanche airfield, having crossed the sea to continue the struggle, were welcomed as heroes.

And then Pétain spoke out. The old Marshal, whom the frightened politicians had dragged out of his Madrid embassy in order to abandon all powers to him, uttered these fateful words: "The fighting must end." Then came the armistice, most of France occupied by the Wehrmacht, the new government installed in Vichy.

In a few days, in an unsettling, abrupt manner, the enthusiasm that had animated the inhabitants of Algiers subsided. Everyone was thinking of those who would come home demobilized. The new slogans fortunately imposed no sacrifice: "Work, Family, Country." "Let us hate the lies which did us so much harm." "Let us find again our ancestral virtues." Everyone settled into the defeat as if in a pious ordeal from which he thought he would not suffer too much: "I have found some sugar"; and "I, a whole ham": that was the new refrain. My comrades did not consider themselves to be involved. They would say, laughing, "Are you coming to Franco-Beach? We're going to hang our wash on the Siegfried line!"

There was a shock at the beginning of July 1940 when the fleet suddenly pulled up anchor with flags flying. A rumor went around: "The war is not over! It is still going on!" If it had been announced at that time that the Empire was going to enter the struggle, no one would have been surprised. Then more news came: At Mers-el-Kébir the English had fired on our ships, which had refused to join them, and many sailors were dead. There was stupor, incomprehension.

The appeals of de Gaulle had gone almost unnoticed. At our house my father had succeeded very early on in getting the BBC from London, and on June 20 we heard, "France has not lost the war." [Perhaps Mario heard a rebroadcast of de Gaulle's speech of June 18.] De Gaulle's harsh voice, his brusque tone, his manner of speaking seemed antipathetic to me, but the words were those I was waiting for. In the following days jamming made reception almost inaudible, but we still listened eagerly. For me, the truth was there.

I wanted to do something and, despite the general disaffection, two or three of my best friends joined me in this: "De Gaulle must be told that it would not take much for Algeria to enter the war." I decided to go and explain all that at the English consulate on the Boulevard Amiral-Pierre, an antiquated building opposite the Admiralty. I went there and, not noticing the policemen in civilian clothes posted in the arcades at the entrance, climbed the stairs to the office on the second floor. In front of the door were more policemen, and I scarcely had time to read a sign posted on the door — "Consulate closed; for all information see the consulate of the U.S.A." — when one of them demanded, "Where are you going?" I ran down the stairs, shoving aside the men who tried to bar my way. They chased me, but I was thoroughly acquainted with the labyrinth of little streets in the navy quarter.

The consulate of the United States was in the upper section of Algiers, near Galand Park, in a big new building. The orderly wanted me to fill out a form, but I refused. Finally an official came, but when I told him what had happened at the English consulate he replied that it was of no interest to them. When I insisted, he opened the door: "Get out of here or I'll call the police!"

So the summer of 1940 had gone by.

My father, the preceding autumn, had accepted the idea that I should not go to the *lycée* but should take some private courses so as to devote my time to music. ("Take advantage of your remaining time," he said.) Now he thought that I should resume a normal cycle of studies. So at the beginning of October 1940 I found myself back on a bench at the Grand Lycée with pals whom I had left three years before, to live in Paris with my parents and pursue my studies at the Collège Stanislas. From the first days on, the idea of settling in to the school year, when the London radio was calling us to join the Free French, was intolerable.

What could I do? I was not in Brittany, where with a boat and a good wind one could reach England in a single night. If only I knew some aviator! From Oran and Morocco, in the days following the armistice, some succeeded in reaching Gibraltar. Now they were fighting. Others, like my friend Jean Diacomo, were burned to death at takeoff: the controls had been tampered with without their knowledge.

Rachid, a friend at the sea scouts, told me, "I have a relative who is returning to Morocco. I spoke to him, and he agrees to let you go with him; then he'll help you reach Tangiers. You can trust him; he is a Hadj; he has been to Mecca."

In fact, he was a very congenial cloth merchant. With his traditional Moslem costume, his glasses, and his *taboosh* of gray wool, he resembled a Koranic schoolmaster. We agreed on a meeting place for departure; I left a letter at my house, and we met at the Café de la Régence near the big mosque. But when I showed him my identity papers, he informed me that they were now insufficient to get into Morocco. "You must have a special pass from police headquarters, but you have time; I'm not leaving until tomorrow."

At police headquarters, they declared, "You are a minor; your father will have to come to make the request."

Rachid took me over to Government Square and pointed to a fellow seated on a bench, a professional false witness. His name was Benchétrit. He was a jolly old rake, short, about 50; his whole appearance was comical. I sat beside him.

"I need a father."

"You have one, my son; it'll be ten francs."

We went up the stairs of the police headquarters. In the offices people were bustling about, some of them typing. Suddenly "my father" was off at top speed, with policemen after him, shouting, "This time we've got you!"

But Benchétrit lost himself in the crowd, and I, too, disappeared.

Next, I learned that, with a passport, I no longer needed a special pass, so I went to the Préfecture, where again a clerk at the information desk recited, "You are a minor; you must have your father's authorization."

A superintendent who had heard my name approached and said in a friendly tone, "I am a friend of your father; we'll try to arrange things by telephone."

He was already holding the receiver, so I said very quickly, "He is traveling. I'll be coming back with him."

"Fine. Give him my regards."

I hadn't made much progress, and the cloth merchant announced that he could no longer put off his departure. I went back to our villa at Hydra, on the heights above Algiers, and the look my mother gave me, happy over my return and yet dismayed by my sorrow at having failed, comforted me.

This attempt to escape would have appeared preposterous if it had been known to the people of Algiers. The almost religious veneration accorded the Marshal was growing stronger every day. Rare were those who, like us at Mont-Hydra, anxiously followed the stages of the battle going on in the sky over England.

The crushing of our military power by the Wehrmacht had been so sudden and shocking that a swift defeat of the English, who, to the surprise of everyone, were pursuing the war without us, appeared certain. How could the British army, so feeble and so badly trained, resist for any length of time forces that must be invincible, because they had defeated us? The idea of a superior race was making headway among certain people who were proud of their more-or-less Germanic ancestry. It was annoying, though, that the Italians were also our conquerors. When anyone mentioned this, there was always somebody to declare, "The Germans have only scorn for them; their turn will come." And yet everyone's pride was affected, especially because of the Moslems, whose silence and discretion were in a way embarrassing. Luckily the Marshal knew how to say the right thing: "We must accept the defeat as punishment for past mistakes. What it teaches us will serve as the basis for a moral renewal of France."

I went back to the *lycée*, where, because of the distance from home, I was a semi-boarding student. The Grand Lycée, known as the *lycée* of Bab-el-Oued, was at the other end of Algiers, at the foot of the Casbah and opposite the headquarters of the army division, so that it seemed like an army barracks.

It was dark every morning as I left Mont-Hydra and walked quickly to the trolley bus stop a few hundred meters down a little road through a pine forest. Then, during the ride, I passed the places where my first years had been spent. First we crossed the Colonne-Voirol quarter, which got its name from the monument erected there in memory of General Voirol; the place was important because it served as a kind of exit gate from Algiers toward the towns of the interior, Boufarik, Blida, Médéa. We passed the great pines and eucalyptus trees in the Bois de Boulogne and then descended the gently sloping streets leading to the center of the city. At the lower end of the Rue Michelet we were in the flat part, in the gardens of the Boulevard Lafferrière dominated by the war memorial. In front of the main post office I got off the trolley bus and onto a tram that went down the Rue d'Isly toward the Opera and Bresson Square. In the soft morning light the city began to come to life as the arcades of the Rue Bab Azoun passed by. Still another stop at Government Square, a vast forum which, as the center of the city shifted toward the Rue Michelet, was left to the common people. To the left, the cathedral; above that the Casbah; to the right two big mosques, then the Boulevard Carnot, and then the tidal basin of the Admiralty. Finally, to the screeching of the rails, we came to the Rue Bab-el-Oued, which opened onto the Place du Lycée. A crowd of us left the tram and climbed up the great staircase that led to the central courtyard.

At the *lycée* I had found again my best friend from the Collège Stanislas, Roger Rosfelder. We recognized with pleasure that our ideas and plans coincided, and that we were alone, or almost alone, among the three thousand pupils in thinking that way. Portraits of Marshal Pétain were posted everywhere; the cult of this ikon had abolished all will power.

The Jews, numerous in our class, were careful and anxious. They expected something serious to happen. It began very quickly with the abrogation of the Crémieux decree of 1871, according to which they had become French citizens; then came the imposition of quotas in the university and the professions. Several of our professors had to leave the *lycée*.

In the residential quarters, the windows of stores owned by Jews were smashed at night by stones. Those Jews who still came to sit on the terrace of the Lafferrière café or the Coq Hardi were sometimes slapped, insulted, and driven away, and the owners of the restaurants were told to refuse them service.

These stupid racist actions did not have the support of everyone, but those who disapproved were indignant only when speaking to a select few, disarmed as they were by the complicity of the authorities and the reticence of the already censored press. The political tool of anti-Semitism was beginning to take its toll, leading many people from "Marshalism" to

Naziism. Latent anti-Semites, they would not have dared hope for such entertainment a few months earlier.

Sometimes in the evening, when returning home from the *lycée*, I would get off the tram in front of the university to chat for half an hour with my pals at the "Otomatic." While drinking a glass of beer, we would watch the groups walking along the tree-lined sidewalks of the Rue Michelet. They were almost all young people, among them former fellow students. These chaps had never thought of anything but girls and swimming in the sun; now they were transformed into fanatics militating for Naziism. Their admiration for the Germans knew no bounds. They were members of Doriot's party, the PPF, or of the SOL (legionary organizations inspired by Hitler's storm troops). No doubt remote-controlled by the Germans (the Axis armistice commissions were discreet but active and determined to take over North Africa rapidly), they undertook to provoke agitation for the purpose of gaining power, taking control, and leading Algeria to active participation on the side of the Axis.

One evening I was going toward my tram when in the crowd in front of the main post office I saw a group of about 30 of these fellows shouting, "Jews back to the ghetto!" Some of them were punching and beating two young Jews who, their faces swollen and bloody, were trying to run toward the Rue Bab-Azoun. Among the most brutal I recognized Big Roubart, hefty, thickset, known for his bull-like strength but also for his rough simplicity. I went over to him, and in the tumult I took him by the arm and shouted, "Stop pounding on them like that!"

"You're right — my left is no good. A straight-arm with my right does a better job!"

My father had wanted to publish some articles, but they had been censored; now, without gasoline, he almost never left his villa. He had tried to take the trolley bus down into town.

"I will never set foot in it again," he told us on returning home. "I was on the platform beside Colonel Piédalu. Speaking to him of one thing and another, I said, 'They're giving all our wheat to the Germans; the bread we eat is disgusting.' Then this imbecile stirred up the whole crowd, declaring, 'Sir, the Marshal's bread can only be excellent!'"

We had learned that, in Paris, our apartment in the Rue d'Assas had been thoroughly searched by German policemen. They carried off several files of papers and my brand new grand piano.

During this time at the *lycée,* Roger and I little by little perfected our plan to join the Free French. We pored over a map of Morocco. My parents' chauffeur, Mohamed Guédri, a very crafty Kabyle and an old accomplice in my playing hooky at the time that my father was watching me closely, had obtained for me two automatic pistols and ammunition. The weapons came from Gouraya, on the coast between Cherchell and Ténès, where they were landed clandestinely from Spanish feluccas.

I had some money in the savings bank and, having faked a parental authorization, I had withdrawn it. Our schoolmate Yves Bouât was supposed to join us, but at the last minute he had given up the idea. As a Breton, he could not stomach what had happened at Mers-el-Kébir. Guéraud had replaced him.

The door of the cell opened.

"Come out!"

In the office of the police inspector, Guéraud looked at me sadly. "They know everything, Mario."

Superintendent Faux was exultant. "They have confessed! They have confessed! The scoundrels!"

He added, his bloated face suddenly threatening, "We know all that. Now let's get down to serious matters. Where are the weapons?"

"Weapons? We don't have any."

"And we know that you do have some. The train has been searched and nothing was found. So where are they?"

"You searched us too. You know we have none."

Our frankness seemed to have won out. It was 4 a.m.

"Take them to headquarters. We'll resume at eight," said Faux to his inspectors.

At police headquarters uniformed policemen shut us up in the jail, where about 20 Moslems were sleeping on the ground or sitting on benches. The room was dimly lighted by a bulb in the ceiling. The walls were filthy, the odor strong. The only ventilation came from the door with thick iron bars opening onto the corridor. Some Moorish women, no doubt prostitutes, were squatting in a corner. No sanitary installation; urine ran along the tiles. We stretched out on the benches.

Two guards opened the grill and pushed before them a half-starved Moslem. One guard held in his hand two pieces of fennel; the other shouted, "So you steal! You take advantage of the darkness, you bastard! Admit you stole!" At the end of each sentence he struck the Arab on the head with a bludgeon. The guards finally left, and the Arab collapsed in a corner. I dozed off.

The next day they took us to the office of the Mobile Guard inspectors. Sayah was in Faux's office. Daoud, a Moslem, tall, fat, his fez garnet red, was guarding. He stood deliberately away from us, near the window, in order to let us speak to each other.

"We have to escape or things will get worse," Guéraud said to me quietly.

Without turning around, Daoud murmured, "You're out of luck. They are going to shoot you."

Gongora and Constantini, two other guards, were in the next room. They joined us and began to chat. "We're clever people — that's why we caught you," Gongora boasted.

"I don't give a damn."

He did not get annoyed but continued, "You'll understand. Wait a minute."

He left the room and returned with a big register, which he made me read: "Faivre, Marcel Henri, called Mario, 18 years old, 1 meter 76, chestnut hair rather long, light-colored eyes, sailor's sweater with a rolled collar, tan jacket, gray raincoat — trying to reach the Gaullist dissidents, armed, dangerous."

"You see, this was disseminated everywhere. Can you imagine that we wouldn't have got you with all that? A general alert, all ports sealed, ships searched. At Bel-Abbès those imbeciles let you get away; they only had the description of your pal."

Sayah came out of Faux's office and sat beside me. The inspectors went off to telephone.

"Faux is trying to make me talk," said my friend. "He's looking for the weapons. He said to me, 'Tell me where they are, and you are free. I will give you a note for your father saying that you are a good boy.' I told him I hadn't seen any."

We decided to use our traveling money, and we insisted that our meals be brought from the Hôtel Transatlantique. Each time, Superintendent Faux opened the envelope in which our money was being kept, paid, and had me sign a receipt. We invited Gongora and Constantini to share our libations with Mascara wine; we played cards and chatted with them. Faux spoke to us in a friendly manner; he told us that he gave up teaching philosophy for police work. But from time to time, with a crafty remark he tried to pump us.

The telephone rang, and Faux answered it. His tone became very respectful. "No, no treated well; they are here — fine — very well." He hung up.

"You are being turned over to Military Security at Oran."

Then he turned to me. "Your father is arriving tonight."

After our dinner, the inspectors went home. Daoud remained in the next room. Faux came back to keep us company and, as no one except for us was there to witness his Vichyite zeal, he was altogether relaxed. With the affable tone of a professor loved by his pupils, he read us passages from the Penal Code concerning minors; then he went to the station to meet my father.

Soon afterward they arrived, walked down the corridor, and entered Faux's office. The superintendent was carrying my father's suitcase. He shouted to Daoud to have me brought in. I embraced my father and we sat down.

Faux seemed in a good humor. He gave my money supply to my father. "Here is the money. Everything is accounted for."

My father took the envelope and passed it on to me: "It's yours."

In a somewhat sad and skeptical voice he asked, "Did they mistreat you?"

"No."

Together with Sayah and Guéraud we went to the Transat Hotel.

The train stopped at Bel-Abbès. Roger Rosfelder and his father joined us in our compartment, and our two fathers carried on a conversation. Mine was tall, somewhat corpulent, with a wide forehead, long hair down to his neck, precise speech; he was often indignant, often disillusioned. Roger's was of average height, his gray hair cut short; he was active, enterprising. Both expressed the same antipathy for the Vichy regime, my father because of profound philosophical and humanistic convictions, Eugène Rosfelder as a leading adherent of radical-socialism who had just been relieved of his office as mayor of Cape Matifou and replaced by an appointed mayor. In a bad position to plead our case with the authorities, they feared severity in our encounter with the repressive laws enacted by Vichy.

Roger was satisfied. After his arrest, seated between the two policemen who were taking him away in a car, he had succeeded in slipping his rubber bludgeon between the cushion and the back of his seat. Then, left alone for a moment and put in charge of some food, he had attached a sausage to the button of his fly, letting it hang inside his pants. The inspector who searched him was astonished.

How had our adventure failed? At the *lycée*, one of André's pals had lost his nerve and given the alert.

Roger's father turned toward us. "You were lucky they caught you; the *passeurs* would certainly have murdered and robbed you. Others before you have got their throats cut, and without weapons you'd have been done for. But I don't understand, Roger, why you said in your letter, 'Don't have anyone look for us; we are armed and will defend ourselves.' Well? Did you think you would intimidate us?"

At Oran, Military Security was situated in the bastions of an old fort that must have dated from the Spanish occupation. We waited in the inner courtyard while in a nearby office our fathers explained our case as best they could. A door opened and I was called. In the vaulted room were two officers. They were tall, and they appeared direct and serious, frank and decisive.

"So you are the leader?" one of them asked me.

My "Yes" was full of humility. There was no reason to be proud of our failure. They introduced themselves cordially: Captain Glorieux, Lieutenant Schellenberg.

"What were you trying to do?" asked the captain.

"Join Free France to fight the Boche."

"You won't have to go so far. Give us a little time to prepare ourselves."

"What can we do?" I asked in surprise.

"You'll know soon. You're free. Go back to Algiers and keep quiet. You were very lucky this time, but if you do it again we will be unable to do anything more for you."

We shook hands, and I left. The sky was blue.

My father asked me to go back to the *lycée* so that people would know that I was not in prison or in a concentration camp. I was called before the principal, a tall, stout man, affable and respected.

"I congratulate you. Here we perform passive patriotism, and you have performed active patriotism," he told me quietly from behind the thick glasses that seemed to set him apart. I thanked him and reminded him that if such words happened to become known he would run a great danger of being relieved of his duties.

"I know. That's what gives meaning to my words."

After a few days, Roger and I realized that we were back where we had started from. Except for a few sympathizers, most of our comrades considered us somewhat hot-headed. It was true that the English were finding their situation more and more critical. The Wehrmacht seemed to have given up for the moment its plan to invade the British Isles, but the Luftwaffe had undertaken a war of attrition, with the night-time bombardment of industrial centers and cities. Londoners were dying by the thousands under the bombs. German submarines were sinking many of the English ships that were attempting to transport necessary armaments and provisions from the United States. German troops occupied Yugoslavia and Greece and landed in Tripoli. Rommel's Afrika Korps came to the aid of the Italians thrown back in disorder by the English. Now the forces of the Berlin-Rome Axis, established in Libya, were directly threatening Cairo.

France seemed devoted to the interests of the conquerors. For the defeated Vichy government the only concern was to make itself a valuable ally of the enemy. It was unique in the annals of history that, in a three-week campaign, we had lost a million and a half prisoners. Almost every family had one or more of its members in a camp in Germany.

For the population of Algeria, the advent of a long reign by Hitler was already an accepted fact. The "National Revolution" was in full swing. It covered with a tricolor veil all that was being done by Vichy: surveillance of public opinion, censorship of the press, interdiction of political parties, anti-Semitic measures, suppression of the trade unions.

The French Legion of Combatants, the special association of military veterans, originally the spearhead of a moral revival, was transformed into an instrument for the diffusion of the Marshalist mystique. Membership, voluntary at first, was rapidly made obligatory with the creation of the "Friends of the Legion," then of the "Volunteers of the National Revolution." From the first weeks that followed its creation, the Legion considered itself to be entrusted with the mission of keeping an eye on the adversaries of the regime. The few government employees who did not join up were dismissed. Soon informing was encouraged. Posters were stuck up in all the offices of the Vichyist associations: "If someone listens to the Gaullist radio, tell your leader." "If you hear someone utter words against the Marshal, tell your leader. It is your duty."

Many Moslems welcomed as a pro-Arab pledge the abrogation of the Crémieux decree and other anti-Semitic measures. They favored the old Marshal. Others secretly supported the PPA, the Algerian Popular Party, which was demanding independence for Algeria. The Italo-German armistice commissions were discreetly behind this movement, hoping to foment disturbances that would allow them to establish themselves more solidly in North Africa on the pretext of restoring order. None of the Frenchmen who belonged to the PPF (the French Popular Party), likewise remote-controlled by the Nazis, were at all aware of the duplicity of the occupiers.

For almost all the Europeans of Algeria, Pétain had become a sort of "Bon Dieu." His colored portrait was enthroned in the place of honor in households and in store windows, where it conveniently replaced everything the Germans had carried off. De Gaulle, far off in London, where he was able to assemble only a very few supporters, was considered here only as a deserter, a traitor condemned to death, in the pay of London, which was a hotbed of Jews and Freemasons.

Like everyone else, Roger and I went to the beach, but we did not give up the idea of joining Free France. At the sea scouts, we had a trawler in good condition, the *Primauguet*. If we could succeed in reaching the open sea, we would almost certainly be picked up by one of the boats of an English convoy, which followed the coast 20 miles out, loaded with supplies for the English army in Cyrenaica. Other people, leaving from Oran, had already tried and succeeded.

Movements in the port of Algiers were closely supervised. Except for a few merchant vessels that still sailed at reduced speed, burning coal scraps in their engines, only fishing boats were authorized to go out, and they had to be back before sunset. The national navy was watching. The passageway was closed by a row of barges tied together, to which was anchored a steel antisubmarine net. For passenger boats and freighters, a tug opened and closed this floating dam. Small boats went out on the left, along the jetty near the Admiralty pier, through a narrow passage a few meters wide, guarded and closed at night.

I was registered for service in the navy, as was Madjib, Rachid's brother. We decided to equip the *Primauguet* for fishing. We would begin by making a few honest sorties; then, some foggy evening, with provisions on board, Roger and I and two other friends would make a run for the open sea. We agreed to say nothing about it to Rachid. Ever since he had gone to congratulate my father on the occasion of a cultural lecture that my father gave at the Pierre-Bordes Hall, Rachid was capable of running to tell him everything, to make himself interesting.

On May 8, 1941, Madjib and I went with our navigation documents to the maritime registry situated at the Admiralty, a few meters away from the office of the sea scouts. We came out with the *Primauguet*'s registration entirely in order. Almost every day we went to sea in order to make ourselves more familiar with the controls. Naturally I was no longer going to the *lycée*. A good thick evening fog, and we would have tricked everyone.

On May 26 I was ordered to appear at the maritime registry.

"Give me your navigation documents."

"Here you are."

"We are keeping them. You are grounded. Give us the *Primauguet*'s registration."

"Why?"

"Don't ask any questions. It will be better for you."

Once again, we were deeply disappointed. Furthermore, we understood that, if we continued, we would find ourselves behind the barbed wire of a concentration camp.

Rachid reasoned with me: "Why do you keep trying to leave when you are so well off here, with such good parents? Let others make war. It is God's will. If you say no to Him, you'll only make trouble."

Rachid had two cousins, girls, who lived in a house at Saint-Eugène, a peaceful quarter in the western part of Algiers, beyond Bab-el-Oued. Sometimes their parents went to spend a few days on their farm at the foot of the Atlas Mountains near the little village of Arba. One evening, we knocked at the door of the villa, in a little street near the sea, and Rachid's aunt opened the door. Under the arcades of the patio the old uncle was listening to his phonograph, his ear up against the horn. R'daouich (Buttercup) was 17, Rachida 16. The two sisters were very pale, because they never went out without veils. We chatted together. They spoke perfect French, without a trace of an accent, as up to the age of 13 they had been in a Catholic convent. One of them went to the piano and played a *touchia*. I played too, and they were delighted. R'daouich, needle in hand, was embroidering the thousands of arabesques that would adorn her wedding gown. We drank mint tea. It was night when Rachid and I caught the last tram.

At the end of June, my father asked me to drive a herd of mules from one of his farms near Mouzaïville to our estate at L'Aïn-Hamadi, on the shore between Ténès and Mostaganem, and to stay there awhile to take care of the farm work. Roger went with me, and five Moslem employees whom I knew well took care of the animals. We traveled at night on horseback, under a starry sky; during the day we slept in the shade of the pines or swam in the creeks. A few days after we arrived, our good friend François Hérelle, called Kiko, who was our age, and his 17-year-old sister, Germaine, joined us. Our house was surrounded with fragrant maritime firs, pines, and fig trees. In front of us was the shore, and out to the horizon stretched the sea. No electricity, no news; we lived by fishing and hunting. When it was windy the wild game did not come out, nor did the fish; then we lived on crab soup and the first grapes.

Toward the end of the last century, in 1871, a few colonial families settled on this shore and at the foot of the wooded hills of the Dahra. They were deportees from the Commune whom Elie Reclus, a libertarian intellectual and brother of the geographer Elisée Reclus, had managed to gather there. They created small farms with very simple buildings and started cultivating this land of refuge, together with the Moslem Berbers of the neighboring villages. Their descendants, the Régniers, the Lecomtes, the Cotinauds, the Nobles, carried on their rustic existence with biblical customs, far from the anger of the gods. The individualistic philosophy of Elie Reclus remained in their hearts, and although they were tolerant people their pacifism remained firm. They avoided violence and tried to shield themselves from government intrusion into their existence. Educated and cultivated, they read a great deal. My father's works shared their bookshelves with the *Ballade des dames du temps jadis*, with Voltaire, Dostoevski, Giono.

At Christmas time in 1940, I had come to spend a few days at L'Aïn-Hamadi and had had an opportunity to become deeply aware of the right of these people to remain apart from the upheavals of the world from which they had withdrawn. On a beautiful sunny afternoon, hoping to improve the ordinary diet of the farm, I had taken my rifle and, on my faithful horse Négro, had made my way to a little abandoned fort surrounded by pine trees on a hillock overlooking the shore. Climbing over the tumbled-down walls around the courtyard, which was overrun with absinthe and witches-claws, I had taken a position facing the sea, behind one of the loopholes, to wait for doves to pass by. Suddenly, coming from the east, the hum of an airplane grew louder. The next moment, right at my level and almost touching the fort, the huge bulk of a trimotor Junker 52 appeared. With lightning speed, at the sight of the swastika I had fired. Without changing course, the big German plane had gone away toward the west.

On the way back to the farm on my black horse I was far from congratulating myself. To be sure, with a number four bullet I could not have done any harm to the Junker, but one of the passengers had perhaps seen me through one of the portholes when I had swept my gun up to my shoulder, aimed, and fired. To satisfy my desire to fight Naziism and my refusal to accept defeat, I had risked bringing trouble to this little community, whereas in different circumstances I would have done everything to protect it. That episode strengthened my desire to join the Free French forces, volunteers fighting far off under fictitious names to avoid reprisals on their loved ones. Naturally I remained silent after the incident. Not that I imagined that the Germans on the Junker were busy counting the holes in their rudder, but so as not to create a climate of anxiety or provoke a lot of talk with unfortunate consequences. On my return to the farm I had simply announced, "I missed a big wood pigeon."

Indolently stretched out in the sun on the beach at L'Aïn-Hamadi, Kiko, Roger, Germaine, and I took inventory of our successive failures while watching the warm sand slide through our fingers. Sometimes we gazed for a long time at the debris of airplanes, cast up by the sea, on which we could read English writing.

Kiko's and Germaine's father had died a few months earlier. In order not to abandon his mother, Kiko had given up participating in our plans, but neither he nor his sister was accepting the French defeat, Naziism, the hypocrisy of Vichy. In the evening, in the light of the oil lamp, we talked.

Our principal hope now lay in my brief conversation in Oran with Captain Glorieux and Lieutenant Schellenberg. I couldn't remember it with absolute exactness. Did they say, "Get ready; we will warn you"? Or simply, "You will be warned"? No, they clearly let it be understood that we would receive instructions at the proper time. Yes, but when? I was sure of one of Captain Glorieux's sentences: "We are gathering our armament and then we will begin." Well then, while waiting, we too had to get organized. We agreed that, once back in Algiers, we would begin to form cells with a few absolutely dependable comrades and to recruit others, but very carefully, for the ground was shaky. We would have to search out those who shared our ideas and who would be capable of acting and keeping quiet when the time came.

My friends left, and in mid-September I went back to Algiers by way of Orléansville, to see Mohamed Sayah. He and his cousin Maamar were going to recruit some of their friends discreetly. "Not more than five or six; later on we'll see about more," I told them. From time to time Sayah was to come to Algiers to see how things were going.

The autumn of 1941 arrived. I worked on my "philo" and music. Yves Bouât, who had for a while considered going with us last March to Morocco, was now at Toulon. A Breton, he had enlisted in the navy. As for Roger, Kiko, and myself, through contacts, with information from friends, we were spinning our little spider's web. A sympathizer would take us to someone who was ready to act and, through approaches and conversations, we would sound out the possibilities and on one pretext or another maintain contact. We made sure periodically that feelings or determination had not changed, and we avoided giving the impression that we were recruiting for a coup, or putting recruits in touch with others they had not already known. The results were rather modest, but we hoped that if favorable events should take place our enterprise would snowball.

Opinion in Algiers had not changed. Day after day the radio and press announced Rommel's successes in Cyrenaica, where the British 8th Army was defending itself desperately before Benghazi. The entrance of the Germans into a war with Russia and the overwhelming advance of the Wehrmacht toward Moscow had fanaticized even more wildly those committed to collaboration. The masses waited smugly. We would have been denounced at the first move.

Guédri, our chauffeur, got me a nine-shot 7.65 automatic pistol, a good weapon. He could no longer count on the supply route through Gouraya, as the coasts were well guarded: an organization of *couairs*, Moslem auxiliaries with European officers, had been reinforcing the surveillance of the coast for some time.

We made a discovery that significantly improved our possibilities. On our neighbor's estate, hilly and covered with big pines, was an underground tunnel, which we knew about because we had often explored it when we were children. You could enter at two places fairly far apart, hidden by bushes. While making a new exploration, Roger and I noticed that someone had built two walls shutting off a section about 40 meters long. That intrigued me, all the more because my sisters had noticed a coming and going of military trucks covered with tarpaulins, during the days following the armistice. With a crowbar wrapped with rags to deaden the noise of the hammering, I made a little hole in one of the walls, while Roger kept watch. We were under our neighbors' house and could hear them moving the furniture as they cleaned house. About 20 centimeters under the first hole I gouged out another of the same size (two or three centimeters); then I put my eye to one of the holes, with the bulb of the flashlight shining through the other. The vault was full of boxes of weapons, no doubt hidden from the armistice commissions. On each crate the contents were listed in black letters: 60-caliber mortars, 60-caliber projectiles, machine guns, munitions. There appeared to be no cases of rifles, automatic weapons, pistols, grenades, which would have interested us more, but the find was really fantastic. With a wad of bread and some dust we carefully filled up the holes and told no one but Kiko about it.

Should our groups go directly into action against the armistice commissions? The Germans and Italians were waiting for just that, so they could increase their troops and their control in North Africa. Against the Vichy regime? Not having precise enough information, we would risk targeting people who, in secret, were pursuing the same goals as we were. The PPF or the SOL? We didn't even consider it. Those people were annoying, but there were a few good men among them who might join us. Some of them were already providing information without knowing it. We decided to wait while continuing to gnaw away underground, like ants.

At home at Mont-Hydra, Sundays went on very much the same. Our house was vast. Of Moorish style, it overlooked a great park planted with pines, eucalyptus, cypress, palm trees. Under the trees were paths bordered with cineraria and iris in alternating shade and sunlight. A little orange grove, some lemon trees, pomegranates, and almonds grew near the road below. To the east we could see the bay, the low green point of Cape Matifou, the blue mountains of the Kabylie.

Beginning about eleven in the morning, friends of my father would arrive, almost all of them artists, writers, painters, journalists. In the sunlight of the park they conversed until time for our noon meal, at which about a dozen of us would assemble. In the afternoon a few others joined this small group, and the conversations continued into the evening, in our big living room. Some of the visitors were still young, others had gray hair, but all had kept alive the liberal and individualistic spirit of Algiers of the last century — Algiers, which was the first and almost the only city of France to follow the example of the Paris Commune in 1871. They came to see my father, the writer Marcello-Fabri, President of the Algerian Federation of Intellectual Workers, in order to immerse themselves again in an atmosphere of lively discussion. My father had chosen this pseudonym, Marcello-Fabri, the translation into Esperanto of the name Marcel Faivre, in 1907, when his first collection of poems appeared. He was 18, and it was a time when hopes for a universal peace were growing. Later he kept this name of a citizen of the world as an act of faith in the future brotherhood of man.

In the afternoon, friends of my older brother, Gérard, and of my sister, Geneviève, slightly younger than I was, arrived. They were almost all university students, and they set up a dance floor in the dining room. My friends, Roger, André, Kiko, and two or three others, formed a separate band in company with my sister Monique, who was 16, and her friends from the Milly boarding school.

One afternoon, for our amusement, Roger and I fought a duel with swords in front of our house. The girls formed a circle around us, entranced by the spectacle. Suddenly Roger let his sword fall: his wrist was wounded and he was bleeding profusely. Professor Henri Jahier, a friend and disciple of my father, was there, and he took Roger to the nearby Clinique des Orangers and gave him a dozen stitches; Roger woke up in a little white room where he stayed for the next two days. His parents remained polite but seemed a little strained. A few days later Roger reappeared with his arm in a sling. I gave him my 7.65 as a present, and he was so pleased that he made me a gift of his watch. His mother, who was clearly not informed about the 7.65, said, "Well, Roger, I don't understand. Mario wounds you and you're the one who gives him a watch."

Now a question arose: should we contact Captain Glorieux and

Lieutenant Schellenberg to inform them what progress we had made and ask for directives? That could carry heavy consequences if we were being watched, or if they were. The initiative had to come from them. We decided to wait some more.

It was winter. On the high desert plateaus in the southern Atlas, the internment camps had multiplied: Bossuet, Méchéria, Boghar, Berrouaghia, Djarft, Adjerat M'Ghil. Over there, for racial or political motives, men and women were dying in the icy winds behind barbed wire, the victims of torturers who were neither Germans nor Italians. In the place of honor was posted a portrait of the Marshal, and every morning they raised the tricolor flag.

Pillafort

I WAS SITTING AT A TABLE with a *demi* of beer in the Brasserie du Coq Hardi; it was February 23, 1942. I was waiting for Roger, who was at that moment 50 meters away at the Brasserie Lafferrière. These two establishments were on the Rue Michelet in the most central section of Algiers. The Coq Hardi, close to the university buildings, catered especially to students, while the more important people met at the Lafferrière (the Laf), which faced Lafferrière Square across from the main post office; many at the Laf had their own bridge tables. As was common with the great cafés of Algiers, the terraces encroached extensively on the sidewalks, even surrounding the trees planted there. The tables were protected by zinc awnings through which openings were cut for the tree trunks. In winter the cafe was heated, separated from the street by glass panels.

In these last few weeks the war had changed course. On December 7, 1941, the Japanese attacked the United States at Pearl Harbor and destroyed a large part of its fleet. Now they were having one success after another. America was suffering defeats, but a few months from now her enormous potential would begin to weigh heavily in the balance. In Russia the Nazi troops passed the Dnieper, and Leningrad was besieged. But, contrary to all expectations, the Wehrmacht had not taken Moscow and was experiencing a terrible winter. The Americans and the British were beginning to organize great convoys to supply the Soviet army from the north. Close to us, in Cyrenaica, Rommel, in spite of the prowess of his Afrika Korps, had not been able to cross the Egyptian border. The British troops were being reinforced little by little and, despite the losses inflicted on the convoys by the German navy, were receiving powerful equipment from the United States. In metropolitan France a few men and women, risking torture and death, were organizing clandestine networks to fight against the occupiers.

In a zone called "free," the government, directed by Admiral of the Fleet François Darlan, the Marshal's designated successor, was collaborating more and more closely with the Germans, who were continuing to strengthen their influence and their presence. In Algiers, Vichy was omnipotent, omnipresent, and the brainwashing of the population was actively pursued. In letters six meters high, on the north jetty, the new slogan stood out: "With the Legion or against France." It accurately reflected the state of mind of the vast majority: not to have confidence in the Marshal was to be a traitor to our country.

The day before, our friend Suzanne Grammont had turned 17. Her grandmother gave a big reception, and Roger, Kiko, Germaine, my sisters, and I were there. Suzanne's mother was called Poulet. We were slightly related, two of her sisters being married to two of my mother's cousins. Poulet's second husband was a senator who had been a cabinet minister several times. She was a courageous, unusually outspoken woman who could not stand the prevailing spinelessness.

I had left rather early with my sisters. When the reception was nearly over, Poulet took Roger aside, confiding, "I must introduce Mario and you to an incredible guy who has just arrived in Algiers. With him, you might be killed but you will have done some extraordinary things."

She arranged for us to meet at seven the next night at the Lafferrière. As I somewhat mistrusted vague words tossed out at the end of a party, I asked Roger to reconnoiter first. Now I could see him coming back to the Coq Hardi.

"It's okay. You'll be pleased."

We crossed over to the Lafferrière. At the back of the café there he was, leaning against the bar, a bit stout, solid, with a broad open face, chestnut hair combed straight back, simple and friendly, in a green polo shirt under a brown jacket.

"Mario, this is Captain Pillafort," Poulet informed me. We seated ourselves around a table. I felt completely confident, and we approached the subject directly. Alfred Pillafort, smiling, affable, spoke easily. He knew about what we called the Tlemcen interlude, and the business of the duel, which Poulet had told him about, pleased him. He had arrived a few days earlier, having embarked clandestinely in Marseille, hidden in a refrigerator of the S.S. *Governor General Grévy*. In Algiers they did not dare arrest him, but he had just now been put on an unattached status. He was convinced that the war was approaching a major turning point and that North Africa would play an important part in it.

"We must at any cost prevent it from sinking into the Axis orbit and prepare for a return to the struggle on the side of the Allies," he told us. He had made up his mind to act decisively, and he needed young men who were equally determined. I quickly explained to him what we had done so far, and we agreed to meet the next day, when I would fill in the details.

Roger came with me to the trolley bus stop opposite the Laf. "If he's a traitor, we'll shoot him," he said, "but I have an idea that this time we are on board the right train."

Pillafort was staying at the Hôtel des Etrangers, on the Rue Dumont d'Urville. We usually met on the terrace of the Tantonville, the big café near the palm trees in Bresson Square. This was the meeting place for people from all sections of the city, where citizens of all persuasions would discuss their business, while the muted tol-de-rols of the municipal orchestra drifted across the square.

Often Poulet was there. Whenever Pillafort was late, we talked about him. He was 36, a graduate of Saint-Cyr. As a young lieutenant in the Moroccan *spahis* during the Riff war, he had performed some extraordinary deeds. At 26 he was made Chevalier de la Légion d'Honneur by General Henri Giraud, after having succeeded in surrounding and then killing the brother of the Roghi Belkacem in a sword fight. In 1939 and 1940 he commanded the motorized "Pillafort squadron," and after some fierce fighting in Belgium he found himself behind the German lines. With a few survivors he succeeded in escaping encirclement by crossing the Seine near Honfleur, first by swimming and then by catching a drifting rowboat. A few months ago, while in Cairo, he had run into one of his English friends, Colonel Winttle of the RAF, attached to the Intelligence Service. Winttle's mission was to get to Vichy to try to meet Admiral Darlan, to explore the possibility of a secret accord between England and the Vichy government. Pillafort went with him, and through intermediaries they obtained some assurances, but then Winttle was arrested as soon as he revealed his identity. Pillafort succeeded in arranging his escape, and they hid for a few months in Poulet's Château de Brégançon, in the Lavandou. Then Winttle succeeded in getting over the Pyrenees, while Pillafort made his way to Algiers, where he was now on the army's stand-by list.

Roger, Kiko, and I received our call-up for the first week of March: they were to join the Chantiers de la Jeunesse; I was to go to the Siroco Center, since I was signed up for naval training. At first glance that interfered with our plans and we considered getting university deferment for these eight months of training. But after having talked with Pillafort we followed his advice: he considered that the training and paramilitary instruction that we would receive would be very useful to us.The Siroco Center was 30 kilometers from Algiers on the other side of the bay at the end of Cape Matifou. I would have to find ways to get away from there as often as possible.

Before my departure, there was still time to systematically organize our 25 or 30 recruits into small cells. In spite of being 16, André Rosfelder would take charge of some of them; Germaine would stay in contact with the others. I put my friend Bernard Pauphilet directly in touch with Pillafort. Bernard and I knew each other from Paris days, when we lived in the same building. An officer candidate in the 65th Artillery Regiment on the Mareth line at the time of the armistice, he preferred to finish his law degree in Algiers in order to be as far away as possible from the occupiers. With his friend Arguillère he had already organized a small group of reserve officer candidates.

Pillafort expected to make contact shortly with Glorieux and Schellenberg. To replace Mohamed Sayah, who had impulsively enlisted in the navy, I summoned his cousin Maamar to Algiers and put him in charge of the Orléansville sector. I introduced him to Pillafort, who attached great importance to the participation of Moslems in our enterprise.

Pillafort could not forgive the men of Vichy for having abandoned the struggle while our Empire and navy were still intact. "It is more than cowardice, it is stupidity," he said. "We agreed to lay down our arms at the beginning of a war. At the present time the Empire no longer exists except through the authority that the Boche allows us, and one of these days the Boche will lose the war."

The arms depot in the underground tunnel interested him very much, and he was anxious that, before leaving for the Siroco Center, I make sure everything was still there. In his room at the Hôtel des Etrangers, he took an automatic 6.35 pistol out of a drawer. "I have two weapons, my army revolver, which Winttle gave me, and this one. Take it; it's yours."

The next night I went to the tunnel. Nothing had moved.

On the morning of March 5, 1942, having presented myself according to my call-up order at the Admiralty dock, I took my place among the other maritime recruits of my contingent aboard the armed launch *Angèle Pérez*. We crossed the bay and landed on the wharf of the little port of Lapérouse. A hundred meters from there the buildings of the Siroco Center formed a line under the eucalyptus trees. A moment later, in column formation, with our suitcases in our hands, we went through the gate.

The Siroco Center, on the extreme end of Cape Matifou, was run like a ship. Larboard watch, starboard watch, main wardroom, mid-wardroom, a bell to strike the hours. It was a school for marines but, because of the clauses of the armistice, we had no weapons. Our uniform resembled that of the national navy, but we had only two white pipings on our blue collars (Mers-el-Kébir and Dakar, the second mates told us), and our bérets had neither ribbon nor pompon.

On our arrival we were immediately taken in hand. We attended classes in the strictest discipline. The teaching staff was competent in general but the spirit that reigned in the center was sectarian: only the navy existed, there was nothing good except the navy; our navy had never been dishonored; she resisted at Mers-el-Kébir and Dakar; she was ready to repulse all of the attacks of the hated English or the hated and despised Gaullists. We marched in step twice a day for the raising and lowering of the colors, singing in chorus songs like "Fanchon," or others imitated from German marching songs. In the evening there were meetings, anti-English lectures, anti-English songs.

The young maritime enrollees from the Algerian coast were rather passive; they seemed to be interested only in the end of their training period. Everyone who came from metropolitan France gave the impression of being completely at home in this atmosphere. Among them were about 30 unassigned officers in training for the merchant marine, or first mates from ocean liners, or engineering officers.

For three weeks I was unable to leave the center. Finally, with a bike that André Rosfelder loaned me, I was able to speed off to Algiers where I saw Pillafort again. Everything was normal; more contacts had been made.

My class sessions ended, and I was attached to a group that would have leave only on Sunday. I presented myself to Ensign Devigot, the second in command.

"I have been told that supplying the center is accomplished by specialized mule drivers who drive the carts. I am fully experienced with draft animals, and I'd like to be attached to that squad."

It so happened that they needed someone, and Davigot accepted. There were eight of us mule drivers, almost always on the move, driving one of the four *arabas* or the baggage wagon. Except for me, they were all Corsicans. The stable was located at the little harbor of Lapérouse below the center; we had about a dozen mules to care for, harness, and feed. The work was not disagreeable. Every morning we had written orders, to go to Maison-Carrée or to Hussein-dey to get provisions, to carry washing to the laundry, to bring back barrels of muscatel for the mid-wardroom. After a few altercations with the Corsicans I befriended them. By preference I took the baggage wagon, in which I could hide my bicycle and civilian clothes, and as soon as we got to Maison-Carrée, while my comrades were loading meat at the slaughterhouse, I sped off to Algiers. They didn't ask me where I was going. Their silence was a good sign, but I did not try to enlist them. In a few weeks they would be released, and they were counting the days that separated them from their island.

At the Tantonville or at the Hôtel des Etrangers I met Pillafort's friends, who became mine, among them Raphaël Aboulker, a young Jewish doctor, and his brother Fanfan, members of a family well known and highly esteemed, in spite of the prevailing racism. They were patiently laying the groundwork, recruiting, multiplying contacts, prudently weaving a solid network. A former member of the Etampes patrol, Camille Davidau, a flight lieutenant 45 years old, had been ordered by Colonel Fey, an air force officer sent to Algiers by Vichy for that purpose, to watch Pillafort by becoming his friend, and to send detailed periodic reports. Davidau, who had been with Pillafort in Syria, immediately told him what was going on. When Fey came to Davidau's place to receive a report, Pillafort stood on the garden terrace behind the shutters and listened.

At the Siroco Center my superiors held me in high esteem. I was chosen with about 40 others for a three-month training period at the Ecole des Cadres, the center's staff school at Jean-Bart, a little to the east of Cape Matifou. It was a large villa on the cliff overlooking the beach. Almost all of the trainees were already officers in the merchant marine, and the training was intense. Before dawn we were given a "cleaning up" that lasted about an hour: physical exercises, obstacle courses, diving, swimming, swimming under water among the rocks while carrying a block of stone, rock climbing. Then came courses in navigation with notebook, blackboard, and exams. In the afternoon, at sea, there were long races in whaleboats or in sailing launches. In the evening we sang the customary songs: "On the sea to beat the English." At the end of the month an exhausted comrade contracted pneumonia and died. They relaxed the rhythm a little. I was in very good shape.

My fellow trainees often talked about the Germans, some of them with the confiding tone of a girl who has stupidly let herself be raped, by a virile guy who had appeared to be "proper" in every respect. Others didn't like them but, whether it was prudence or sincerity, it was in their anglophobia that they were the most virulent. I stayed out of these talkfests, for it was not in my plans to stagnate in a cell of Fort d'Estrées.

Sometimes on the horizon we saw a convoy of English ships making their way to Benghazi. Then the batteries of Cape Matifou would begin to thunder and rage like big mongrels bent on showing their hostility. Out of range, the English ships held to their course.

Once when I saw Pillafort, his customary joviality seemed to have been replaced by a somber and dejected frame of mind. "We're standing still," he said, "and meanwhile the other side is organizing the return of France to the war on the side of the Axis. Pretending to respect the armistice agreements which leave it up to France to keep her Empire together, the Vichy minions in North Africa are preparing to repulse any attack 'wherever it comes from': that means any Anglo-American attempt to secure bases for the eventual liberation of Europe. Then, to show the Germans and Italians that we don't need them to defend us, we find ourselves at war on their side. The army of North Africa is being prepared in this spirit and it now has several armored regiments. Laval has just replaced Darlan at the head of the government in Vichy, and his first speech on the radio leaves no mystery as to his intentions: 'I hope for Germany's victory.' But Darlan, who is still Pétain's designated successor, is even more pernicious than Laval — he's more technical in his collaboration. He's secretly helping to supply the Afrika Korps and he's doing everything he can to lead us gradually from collaboration to cobelligerence. General Juin, who was a prisoner in Germany, has become the commander in chief in North Africa, freed by the Germans. Was there a secret agreement? In any case, at a banquet of German and French officers Juin raised his glass to 'our leader, the most prestigious of all, Marshal Rommel.' So where does that put us?"

Pillafort showed me a newspaper: on the first page Admiral Darlan, on a visit to Algiers, was shown embracing the Germans of the armistice commission.

"If we have to, we'll join de Gaulle, but we will fight the Germans," Pillafort declared.

At the Siroco Center our training period at the Ecole des Cadres was ending. Three days of examinations and then the ceremony of conferring the "braids" of squad leaders. I went to the office of Lieutenant Thévenet, commander of the center.

"I've heard that things aren't going well with the mule drivers. I'd like to be able to reorganize this service."

They created the post of muleteer in chief in my honor, and in a few days I assembled a good squad of Corsicans. Everyone was satisfied; there was even an agreement that our uniforms would be changed twice a week. I organized the work so that I could spend almost three days a week in Algiers, where the climate had changed.

Hope was here at last, solidly here; we could count on the events we had been awaiting for so long. Pillafort was exultant; he had succeeded in contacting at the highest level those who had for two or three months been actively preparing for North Africa to resume the struggle on the side of the Allies. He had also established contact with the consulate of the United States. In that month of August 1942 the great dream that we had cherished for so long, the landing of the Americans at Algiers, had ceased to be just an idea.

In the city there was no general change in attitudes, but a few people were beginning to see that an Axis victory was no longer certain. In Libya,

where the British forces were now way superior in number and equipment
to those of the Berlin-Rome Axis, Rommel was experiencing reverses and
had to draw back to the Tunisian border. News of the difficulties of the
Wehrmacht in Russia was seeping through, in spite of the strict censorship.

However, we had to remain vigilant. The attitude of the supporters of
collaboration was hardening. They too were preparing for the coup which
they foresaw as inevitable and were not thinking of turning their batteries
around but rather of hastening the event that would bring Vichy into the
war on the side of the Axis. In a few weeks Axis troops, in a massive west-
ward retreat in Tripolitania, would try to withdraw behind the Mareth line
in the French protectorate of Tunisia. How could Laval, as head of a Vichy
government totally engaged in a policy of collaboration, give the French
army of North Africa an order to open hostilities at the Tunisian border
against forces that he considered to be allies? Only the successful landing
of American troops could prevent this disaster. What was about to happen
would be decisive and would have incalculable consequences.

Without revealing the progress of our enterprise, I took over the little
groups formed some months before. There were some new recruits and an
air of determination, but still in a very closed circuit. There were so few
people in Algiers ready to take part in a pro-Allied conspiracy that contacts crisscrossed very quickly. A fellow identified as "good" would be
recruited by two groups unaware of each other. I was myself the object of
multiple approaches from comrades who I knew were connected to the
organization but who were unaware of my role and kept after me. It could
not go on indefinitely, but each day we were making progress.

One Sunday morning, on leave for a day, I was just arriving at Mont-
Hydra when my sister said that someone wanted me on the telephone. A
voice with a distinguished tone asked, "Do you remember when you were
in Oran?"

"Yes, of course."

"Then, at 1600 be on the terrace of the Tantonville. You will recognize
me; I am an officer in the Chantiers de la Jeunesse, and I will have in front
of me a newspaper folded horizontally."

Was it a coincidence? I was supposed to meet Pillafort at the Tantonville that afternoon.

Discreetly, before going up to him I looked at the man who had
arranged this meeting. He had the appearance of a Spanish grandee. With

his long legs nonchalantly crossed, he was reading a newspaper folded horizontally. I saw from his shoulder strap that he was an officer of the highest rank in the Chantiers. I introduced myself, and in a serious voice he told me that he was a friend of Glorieux and Schellenberg and that he had been an officer in Military Security in Oran not long before.

"The time for action is near, and I'm going to put you in touch with the person who will be your immediate boss."

I was beginning to understand, for I had caught sight of Pillafort a few tables away. He too understood, and now he came over to us. "If it is Mario you want to introduce me to, I warn you that we have been working together for many months."

All three of us laughed. That is how I first met Henri d'Astier de la Vigerie.

I learned that the head of the Chantiers de la Jeunesse, Colonel Jean Van Hecke, was supporting us secretly with everything in his power. Henri d'Astier had become his adjunct, gaining the freedom of action necessary for his secret activity as general coordinator, the key to the entire organization. With the travel orders that Van Hecke got for him, he could move about in all of North Africa quickly and without arousing suspicion. I must never utter his name or mention his existence to anyone whatever, but it was absolutely necessary that contact be maintained if Pillafort should be interfered with. Furthermore I could establish a more discreet system of liaison between them than these conversations at a brasserie table. D'Astier lived nearby, in the Hôtel Terminus.

My posting at the Siroco Center was about to end. In my last conversations with the officers of the center I realized that, in spite of the rigidity of their ethic and their moral isolation, a change was in the air. Basically these were fine men who detested the Boche. I hoped that fate would let them fight on the right side.

On October 11, 1942, I was released. On that afternoon a conference took place in Pillafort's room at the Hôtel des Etrangers, with Lieutenant Daridan and Raphaël Aboulker also present. Events were speeding up; action could unfold in a few days, and the weapons of the underground vault could become indispensable to us. As I was unable to leave Cape Matifou because of the final formalities of the program, one of our people,

Marcel Fellus, with two comrades, went at night to find out if everything was still in place. They had a great deal of trouble finding the entrance, and then, having been discovered, they had to disappear. When I inspected the vault later that night, armed with Raphaël's 7.65 Walther, it was empty; the weapons had disappeared without a trace.

It was a great disappointment, but in the following days we were assured by the United States consulate that we would receive American machine guns and automatic rifles. Everyone prepared for the imminent mobilization of the groups.

Roger and Kiko got out of the service two days after me, and each took charge of a group. Thoumazeau and Masson had theirs. Mohamed Guédri had with him seven or eight Kabyles whom I knew personally. Madjib had a small group of Moslems from the Saint-Eugène quarter. Maamar had done good work at Orléansville, but the distance created something of a problem.

A setback occurred. Roger, under strict orders from his father, had to go back to the agricultural school at Sidi-bel-Abbès. His brother André replaced him while at the same time running a group of young people his own age, sons of well-known Algiers families such as Jean Snyers, son of Jean Mazel, the Belgian consul general, and Martinet, nephew of the painter Albert Marquet. We had to be very careful of idle talk. These chaps expected to participate in an attack on the Germans, but they knew nothing at all about the planned operation.

One morning I found Pillafort radiant. General Giraud had succeeded in escaping. He was without doubt the one who would direct the operation and take command in North Africa. Precise agreements with the Americans were being worked out. Giraud had been Pillafort's general in Morocco; Pillafort was one of his favorite officers.

De Gaulle was kept out of these preparations. The Americans feared that his presence in Algiers might provoke hatred and opposition.

A meeting of the utmost importance was about to take place. Some American generals were to land secretly from a submarine along the coast, to talk for a few hours with the principal leaders of our organization and to iron out details of the operation. I offered our estate at L'Aïn-Hamadi, but it was too far from Algiers. A friend we could trust, Queyrat, had an estate on the shore between Novi and Gouraya. Pillafort could not take part in this conference, since he was too closely watched. Daridan was finding it more and more difficult to cover for him.

On the night of October 21 the meeting took place as planned near Cherchell, in spite of bad weather and security patrols. The top brass arrived: for the Allies, General Eisenhower's assistant, General Clark, the future commander of the operation; General Limnitzer; and Colonel Holmes; from Algiers, the American diplomats Murphy and Knight. For the French side, General Mast, Colonel Jousse, Henri d'Astier de la Vigerie, Navy Captain Barjot, Colonel Van Hecke, Jean Rigault, Bernard Karsenty.

The accords reached at Cherchell provided for two simultaneous actions. The Resistance agreed to see to the rupture of communications when the time came, to arrest the principal Vichy leaders, and to occupy various army headquarters. The Allies agreed to land commandos to relieve the members of the Resistance that same night, before reprisals from the Vichy forces, whose superiority was overwhelming. The date was fixed. We would know it at the proper time.

The other principal points for the Allied landings were Casablanca, Port-Lyautey, and Oran. Organizations identical to ours, although much less structured, were in place.

The political and economic agreements that went with the plan of action were clearly set forth, to be signed in the coming days by General Giraud, who had accepted the functions of civil and military commander in chief in North Africa, and by Robert Murphy, who was simultaneously consul general in Algiers, personal representative of President Roosevelt, and secret delegate of the British government. [Murphy was Roosevelt's representative but not the consul general.] We already knew that in these accords the Anglo-American Allies gave their word to restore to France complete possession of her metropolitan and overseas territories. In the course of the military operations that they would conduct on French soil, they would not interfere in administrative or political matters. The supreme command of all the Allied armies in North Africa was to be held by General Giraud as long as the Allied troops were not greater in number than the French troops stationed there.

The organizers of this meeting, the culmination of a long preparation, took the name the "Group of Five": Henri d'Astier, Jean Rigault, Jacques Lemaigre-Dubreuil, Jacques [Tarbé] de Saint-Hardouin, Jean Van Hecke.

It was wonderful news. Moreover, the visitors gave our friends a few packages of American cigarettes. Pillafort had a share, and he gave me two packages. When I offered a cigarette to a buddy, it amused me to see him smoke it without having any idea where it came from.

The words "resistants," "commandos," were new to me. The Resistance — yes, of course, we needed a name.

General Charles Mast commanded the Algiers division; Colonel Jousse, responsible for security, was in charge of the city. Within the army, these men were virtually alone; they didn't have a single unit or a single platoon to bring to our side. If they came under any suspicion, they would instantly be relieved of their posts.

We estimated our possible numbers at about 700 to 800 volunteers. Opposite us were 11,000 soldiers in Algiers proper, well armed, well trained, with many armored vehicles, reinforced by the armed militia of the SOL, the Legion of Combatants, and Doriot's PPF: about 20,000 armed civilians. Furthermore, the population, subjected for more than two years to intense propaganda, was essentially hostile to us. We were waiting for the arms that the Allies had promised us: 750 Sten machine guns, revolvers, hand grenades, and antitank missiles.

It was a happy time. Pillafort, Poulet, Daridan, and I spent much of the time on the terraces of the Tantonville or the Coq-Hardi; our friends Janon, Marnat, Saint-Blancat, Pauphilet often joined us there. Returning to Bresson Square, we would stop for a moment at the Elysée Couture store, the drop-off point for messages and contacts, to chat with Guy Cohen and his brother Elie. Then we walked on the Rue d'Isly, often without using the sidewalk since there were no longer any autos, for lack of fuel. Only a few trams were running, slowly, in this chloroformed city. We were getting ready without getting excited; we had no doubts.

The last days of October arrived. Fortunately the start of the action was imminent, for it was difficult to keep all of these people reined in for so long without telling them much of anything, and to keep those who knew a little from letting their tongues wag. We had to contend with many attempts at infiltration, as much by the PPF as by certain elements of the police. One attempt was stopped in the nick of time; we came close to disaster. A few weeks earlier, Chief Inspector Bègue had been sent especially to Algiers to attempt to infiltrate informers into our networks and to get at the brains of the organization. The Vichy authorities were becoming more and more anxious to know what was being plotted behind all this careful activity. As their confidence in the police of Algiers was limited, Pierre Laval's cabinet had sent over this policeman, who had broken some rules for the love of a beautiful blonde and who had been given the choice between carrying out a successful mission and dismissal.

Bègue was able to identify a few leaders fairly quickly, among them Saint-Hardouin and Van Hecke. Others were strongly suspected. The eventuality of an Allied landing in North Africa was discovered. Luckily Bègue was unmasked in his turn. Some policemen, friends of ours, understood the goal of his mission and informed us. The immediate execution of this Vichy agent was decided upon. We knew that the few zealots whom he had put in place to spy on us had no contact other than Bègue for passing on their reports. They would have no way to send on their information if their boss disappeared. Pillafort was the one charged with the operation, and he decided that just the two of us should take action, to avoid any leak. The weapon was ready, a sawed-off shotgun which I would carry in a violin case.

On Sunday morning, November 1, he told me to meet him at nine that evening at the Hôtel des Etrangers for a quick last check of details. At 10:30 I was to join him again, and Bègue would be shot down when he went to meet, as he did every evening, his blond mistress, who had followed him to Algiers.

"Get yourself an alibi from 9:30 to midnight," Pillafort directed.

My brother Gérard, without asking for an explanation, got two tickets for a concert that Django Reinhart was to give that evening in the lobby of the Hôtel Aletti. In the afternoon we got his gazogène Peugeot ready in order to have a vehicle available. We had to fill the firebox with wood, light it, and let the gas form, and then we hoped it would run. And that evening we were at the entrance to the Aletti, on the Boulevard Carnot 200 meters from Bresson Square. I met several musicians of the orchestra; if the occasion arose, they would be able to testify to my presence there. My brother, if necessary, would certify that I had not left him.

A little before nine I slipped away to the Hôtel des Etrangers, where Pillafort informed me that the execution was called off. The Group of Five had managed to find out that Bègue had been unable to transmit any precise information concerning our activities. Given the imminence of the landings, the disappearance of Bègue could cause more harm than his continuing with his mission. Furthermore, other policemen who were not hostile to us might become so if one of their own were to be executed. Pillafort and I noted with satisfaction the capability, intelligence, and sang-froid of those who were directing our conspiracy. They had calculated that our chances of survival during the few days that still separated us from action would be better if we followed such a course. So Bègue was able to see his mistress again without interference and, as for me, I spent the evening calmly listening to Django Reinhart.

We were still waiting for the promised weapons, but from November 4 on we could no longer count on them, and Colonel Jousse made arrangements to "borrow" some from army supplies at the last minute. One afternoon Pillafort and I were alone with Henri d'Astier in his room at the Hôtel Terminus, which looked out on the harbor and Bresson Square. We were going over our plans. I asked Henri d'Astier how it had happened that, up to then, we had been able to escape a general dragnet.

"The Vichy people know a lot about us," he told us. "They are hesitating between making preventive arrests or just observing us so as to be more completely informed of the goals we are pursuing. Luckily very few of us know about it, and everyone is keeping quiet because of the general hostility. But what has delayed the dragnet so far is that Laval in Vichy and General Juin and Governor General Yves Chatel in Algiers believe that the Americans can't, from a technical point of view, attempt an operation of any size in North Africa before spring. So they think that if they arrest us now, those who escape from a general sweep might have enough time to reorganize, whereas if they wait until February they'll have more information to dismantle us, and it would be too late then for the few who might escape the dragnet to set up a new organization.

"A diplomatic battle has been going on for several days between Admiral Darlan, who often passes through Algiers these days, and Robert Murphy. Darlan, Juin, and their staffs would like very much to know what the plans are, and they are trying to make Murphy believe that eventually they would be willing to discuss certain problems. But the consul is very sly, and he's still encouraging the Vichy officials to think that the landing will take place someday, perhaps, but not before April or May. Just yesterday, when he learned that the German intelligence service had warned the general staff in Algiers that a large Allied convoy was being formed at Gibraltar, he managed to converse for a moment with a French officer who he knew was an emissary of Juin. Without emphasizing it, he slipped in an allusion to the rapid successes that the Allies are expecting in the eastern

Mediterranean, thanks to strong reinforcements making their way toward Tripolitania. In the frank tones of a Boy Scout, he added, as if letting himself make a slight revelation, that this convoy was passing through Gibraltar and would put in at Malta."

Pillafort and I laughed, glad to know that this chess game, which resembled a flying trapeze, was working to our advantage.

Referring to the interview at Cherchell, the voice of Henri d'Astier became more serious. "It wasn't very easy. The defenders of French interests stood for very little in comparison with the immense power of the Americans that Clark told us about. Fortunately, we have been able to set up a solid organization in the last few months, and some of us occupy key posts. The Allies have to take us into consideration, since we are on the spot, and we are the only ones who can neutralize the forces of the Vichy army during the first hours of the landing. In the course of these conversations, I understood that the Anglo-Americans, even if they weren't sufficiently prepared for such an operation, would have to attempt it. They can no longer resist the formidable pressure from the Soviet general staff to open up a second front at any cost, in order to make the Wehrmacht move some forces toward the west. At Cherchell, we got the impression that the Americans were determined to land, with or without our help, even at the expense of heavy losses and even if they might fail. They have agreed to this with the Russians, who are going so far as to threaten to conclude a separate peace if the promise is not kept. It's lucky that the United States needs us. If fate is with us in this daring coup, we will have prevented the heavy fighting that we don't want, and we will be the ones who inflicted on the Germans their first great reversal."

"Now we can understand the failed landing attempt of the Anglo-Canadians at Dieppe a few weeks ago," observed Pillafort. "Churchill surely knew that he might lose several thousand men and a lot of equipment, without any chance of establishing a beachhead in the west, but he was proving his good will to Stalin. He was gaining time."

"And suppose this affair comes out as it did at Dieppe," I said in turn. "There the failure had few consequences. It was just another battle, English against Germans. Here, the Allies are going to take on the army of Vichy. If they should lose and go back to their ships, it would be worse than anything. In metropolitan France and in the Empire, Vichy's fighting beside the Axis would be celebrated as a victory for eternal France. As for us, our fate would be, with insults in addition, that of the Moslem infantrymen of Maison-Carrée who mutinied in January 1941. Judged in five minutes, with our graves already dug."

In an objective tone, Henri d'Astier answered me: "That might happen, but everything we know leads us to believe that the Anglo-Americans are going to throw everything into it. They can't allow themselves the luxury of just another trick. With the German-Soviet nonaggression pact of August 1939, the Russians made war inevitable. They imagined that the West would exhaust itself in a struggle over several years, and all they would have to do is move into the ruins. The premature collapse of France defeated their plan; with their army intact, the Germans have been able to turn against them. The Soviets would not tolerate a second Dieppe."

"In any case, we intend to go on with it," Pillafort concluded.

The next morning we had some anxious moments. General Mast was afraid that his Indochinese maid had overheard certain conversations and might report them. Pillafort asked me to have the area around the building where the general lived watched, and to give the alert if this woman left. I posted Kiko there and then relieved him at two. At about four o'clock José Aboulker came to relieve me, and I met him for the first time. A brilliant medical student, the son of Professor Aboulker and cousin of Raphaël Aboulker and Bernard Karsenty, he was Henri d'Astier's assistant.

Luckily it was a false alarm. The following day, the sixth of November, Pillafort informed me that, unless there was a counter-order, the landing would definitely be on the evening of the seventh, but I was forbidden to tell anyone whatever, in order to avoid any leak.

Once more we made our calculations. There would be some defections. At the approach of the real coup, some had vanished, but the recruitment had been conducted in such a way that we could firmly count on many of the groups, such as that of the Salle Géo Gras, a physical cultural establishment on Government Square: 50 men at least. They were Hebrews, determined, disciplined, trained. With their backs against the wall, oppressed by the racist laws of Vichy, Jews would furnish about two-thirds of our forces.

On the morning of the seventh, when I had just gotten up, the telephone rang. It was Pillafort. "Come here; I'll wait for you."

A few minutes later I was at the Hôtel des Etrangers.

"It's for this evening," said Pillafort, whose face expressed intense jubilation. "The mobilization of the groups must be complete by 4:30. We'll meet at five at the hotel and go together to 26 Rue Michelet, José Aboulker's place, to receive the first directives."

I began by alerting Kiko, who set off at once, then André Rosfelder, then Thoumazeau, in his bookstore on the Boulevard Saint-Saëns. Meeting time for everyone was 4 p.m., in a spot decided upon several weeks before, an empty vegetable store rented by Guédri's brother, at 18 Rue du Docteur-Trolard, near the bottom of the Rue Michelet.

I had checked the timetables a few days before for trains from Sidi-bel-Abbès and Orléansville, and now I did not try to inform Roger and Maamar: they couldn't get to Algiers in time. I went by tram and trolley bus to the Notre-Dame d'Afrique quarter, where I was supposed to find Madjib, but he was not there, and I lost the rest of the morning looking for him in places where I was told he might be. I went back up to Hydra to inform Guédri, who abandoned his work on his gazogène car and left to carry out his mission.

At noon, at the family table, my father and mother said nothing, but I knew they were anxious. For several days they had realized that something was about to happen, and I felt the weight of their concerned glances.

As soon as lunch was over, I went off again to Notre-Dame d'Afrique at the other end of Algiers and wasted another two hours there. I had just enough time to get to the Rue du Docteur-Trolard at four. As planned, the iron shutters of the store were closed, but I entered through a small door into the hallway of the building. The groups there were calm and disciplined. I could go back to Pillafort.

At five o'clock we were upstairs at 26 Rue Michelet, a stylish apartment house where the Aboulkers lived. It was like a beehive. José hastily introduced people who had been engaged in the same activity for two years without knowing each other: Jean-Jacques Rager, Pierre Barrucand, René Vinciguerra — who had tried to enroll me every time we met, the brothers André and David Cohen — who lived in Hydra. I met Jean l'Hostis, Pierre-Marie Cordier — a young officer in Military Security, and André Achiary — former head of Territorial Security who had been transferred to Sétif and who had returned clandestinely to Algiers. He would be in charge of policemen favorable to our cause and would make the most important civil arrests.

It appeared that there had been quite a large number of defections, especially among those who had learned that the American consulate had not kept its promises and it was going to be necessary to make do with a few hundred old Lebel rifles that Colonel Jousse had managed to lift from the army stocks.

We were about 300 strong, not many but enough to carry out our missions. At six, Colonel Jousse gave us the password to be used between us and the landing troops. Demand: whiskey. Answer: soda. He gave us details on the conduct of the operation, to begin at 10:30 at the Lavaysse garage; he listed the objectives, the groups to be assigned to them, the autos, the buses at their disposal; and he gave out the assignments that had been left to the last minute. It was decided that, among the officers and noncoms brought by Pillafort, Lieutenant Daridan would accompany him; Lieutenant Duquesnoy would remain at the command post to lead the eventual reinforcements, along with Captain Bouin. Bernard Pauphilet would neutralize General Juin, at the head of the group brought by Jean-Jacques Rager. Master Sergeant Gilbert Sabatier would lead the section charged with arresting General Mendigal, commander of the air forces in Algeria.

My groups would be assigned to different missions, railroad stations, the Admiralty, the Winter Palace. I would stay with Pillafort as his second in command. Our objective, with the groups assembled at the Salle Géo Gras, was to seize the headquarters of the XIXth Military Region and General Koeltz, commander of the army corps of Algiers. We were also to occupy and put out of action the army communications center called Central Mogador, through which all military transmissions passed.

Little by little each group leader received his instructions. As he assigned each one his role, Colonel Jousse distributed the official orders signed by General Mast or by himself.

Toward seven, Pillafort and I left 26 Rue Michelet; we would have to be back there at nine. We stopped at the Rue du Docteur-Trolard to tell our groups that they had two hours to eat supper, then went to a little apartment which had been transformed into a hideaway, at 7 Rue Eugène-Deshayes, where Pillafort put on his uniform. We took our weapons, then stopped in for a moment at 10 Rue Michelet, the home of Goéau-Brissonnière, who was giving a dance without suspecting what was going to happen. There we found Daridan and his wife, the Janons, and other friends.

Passing by the Rampe Bugeaud, we noticed large SOL units standing guard in front of the Hôtel d'Angleterre, where part of the armistice commission was staying. It was almost dark, and I mingled with them for a moment to listen to what they were saying. They had gotten wind of a possible attack on the hotel, but obviously they suspected nothing.

Shortly before nine, I returned to the Rue du Docteur-Trolard to tell André, Kiko, Guédri, and his brother-in-law to be at 26 Rue Michelet in a quarter of an hour; they would be able to get the others as needed.

At nine, Pillafort, Daridan, and I were once more at number 26, where more and more people were gathering around a gigantic fish-in-mayonnaise and an abundant buffet. Another conference was taking place on the sixth floor in the apartment of Jacques Brunel, a young lawyer, son of a former mayor of Algiers and brother-in-law of Colonel Jousse. The colonel and I took the elevator together. He was very calm and resolute. But for his uniform, one would have taken him for an academic. He asked me to do everything possible to avoid shedding blood.

Murphy and other American diplomats arrived, and Henri d'Astier spoke with them. This was the first time that I had come face to face with Murphy. He looked typically American: tall, a frank manner but not open enough to draw precise conclusions, with features both soft and deliberate. His clever and knowledgeable look made one quickly put aside the image of a clergyman that he evoked at first sight.

In José's bathroom, transformed into a radio room, messages were being exchanged with Gibraltar and with the Allied fleet, which so far, in order to deceive the combined aerial surveillance of Vichy and the Axis, had stayed well out at sea with their course set for the east, as though heading for Malta. Now that night had fallen, it made an oblique turn toward the south.

Our goals were well defined: to prevent the Vichy forces from engaging in a long and deadly combat against the Allied troops as they landed. General Giraud was supposed to arrive during the night at the Blida airfield, which General de Monsabert, commander of the subdivision, would seize by trickery. Giraud would have in hand the accords signed by himself and Murphy and approved by President Roosevelt, giving France the advantages and guarantees to allow us to re-enter the struggle in an unhoped-for position. André Beyler, an officer of the Chantiers de la Jeunesse who had Van Hecke's absolute confidence, was to receive him.

Achiary had already arrested Delgove, chief of the political police, who, out of curiosity, came up the stairs of number 26. José asked me for two men to guard him while waiting for the central police headquarters to be occupied so that he could be put in jail.

Pillafort, Daridan, and I went to the Lavaysse garage, where Jacques Brunel was directing the distribution of vehicles and the loading of the guns and ammunition, according to plans prepared the night before.

General Mast and Colonel Jousse had had the bright idea of turning against our adversaries an organization that had been created to oppose us: in the provisions of Vichy's permanent orders, the plans for defense in case of a landing provided that the regular army would receive the support of armed civilian auxiliaries chosen carefully for their loyalty to the Marshal; they would wear armbands with the initials "V.P." (volontaires de la Place), stamped with the seal of the general commanding the division. Colonel Jousse had distributed these armbands to us, and we all had one buckled around the left arm. Our military orders had the same origin. Pillafort's orders, which carried General Mast's signature and the seal of the division, read as follows: "In carrying out the measures of the Plan of Protection of the City of Algiers, the group of volunteers A-4 will be responsible for guarding the headquarters of the XIXth Region and the Mogador communications center; the group will relieve the guard post, whose personnel will return immediately to their units." We would thus be supposed to be Vichy volunteers taking part in an alert exercise. These armbands and these military orders would be the keys to open the doors of the city to us.

José asked me for reinforcements to occupy the central police headquarters, and I designated five or six members of my group, among them two Kabyles. Kiko, André, and Guédri were guarding the entrances to the second and sixth floors of number 26, and I sent another group to place themselves under the orders of Captain Watson, a reserve officer of English ancestry, whose enthusiasm and gaiety were a pleasure to see.

Toward eleven o'clock we got into the autos assigned to us and approached the XIXth Region, on Bugeaud Square, where the Mogador transmission center was located. The success of this mission was of the greatest importance. If we failed, the entire opposing military organization would be set in motion and we would be swept aside. If we succeeded, all activities of the armed units, including all transmissions, would be blocked.

Pillafort put on his tankman's helmet with leather padding, as our cars parked in a little street near the XIXth Region. Next, two buses transporting the groups from the Salle Géo Gras stopped in the Rue Mogador, and 50 men climbed out and lined up in two sections, with their rifles on their shoulders.

Leaving one section a little way back to serve as cover, we placed the other about 20 meters from the main gate of the XIXth Region. Pillafort went to the sentinel and asked him to summon the noncommissioned officer in command of the guard. When the latter arrived, Pillafort showed him the order signed by General Mast: the guard was to withdraw to the barracks. The sentinel opened the iron grill, and we directed the first section to march in and take their posts. The sergeant assembled the guard and, marching off in step, they left the XIXth Region. We were "masters of the fortress," to use military parlance.

Those in charge of the groups, Germain Libine, Reserve Lieutenant Jaïs, André Temime, Edmond Benhamou, Roger Morali, and Henri Mesguich, assigned the men of the second section to their positions. With a few others, Daridan and I moved into the interior of the building and arrested the captain on duty.

Pillafort had the concierge point out the apartment of General Koeltz, and when Colonel Jousse arrived they entered the general's bedroom and took him prisoner. From where I was, a few meters behind them, I could see the general in pajamas, beside himself, in a grotesque state of fury. The colonel tried to tell him about the American landing and the resumption of the struggle, but Koeltz was on the verge of apoplexy.

"You did this! You did this! You shall be shot," he shouted in a choked voice.

Colonel Jousse left him to his rage and went out to supervise the progress of the other operations. We organized a vigilant guard so that the general would have no way to escape or to communicate with the outside, and we returned to the courtyard and then to the underground galleries of the Mogador center. Pierre-Marie Cordier had made use of his experience with Military Security to have the protective steel door opened, and one of the groups had captured the personnel in charge of running the place. Jean l'Hostis, a radio specialist, was busy unplugging and disconnecting the communications network. Henceforth no order or request for instructions could be transmitted by the center.

Cordier and l'Hostis left for the civilian telephone centers, and we settled in. It was a beautiful, serene night, almost as warm as summer.

Making the rounds with André Temime, we discovered 12 *spahis* asleep in a guardroom. We took them prisoner and took their weapons; then it was the turn of an adjutant, in whose room we found a machine gun, which we hastily moved to a strategic position.

Civilians and military men began to appear at the main gate, coming to ask why the Mogador center was no longer functioning. We let them come in and took them prisoner. In this manner, General Roubertie, commander of the subdivision of Algiers, his assistant commander, and his Senegalese chauffeur fell into our hands. They were taken down to the underground room now serving as the command post of the center, and put under guard. The other prisoners, officers and transmission technicians, made to sit along a wall in the courtyard, did not react, appearing stunned. A civilian about 30 years old asked me as I passed, "PPF?"

"No, the Americans are landing."

His face froze.

Toward one in the morning the alert sounded; things came thick and fast. Several officers arrived, looking for explanations and orders, and Pillafort explained to them that it was an alert exercise and suggested that they return home to await orders from General Mast. Some left as they had come; others found it strange and aimed their revolvers at us, threatening to fire on us if we did not let them enter. We opened the iron grill half way and took them prisoner as soon as they came through.

Pillafort entrusted me with the responsibility of getting in touch with 26 Rue Michelet, to inform Colonel Jousse of the conduct of General Koeltz, who was incessantly trying to telephone and who had boasted of having thrown a message for the 5th Chasseurs d'Afrique (a light infantry unit) through the window; and also to inform him of the incidents at the main gate.

I left the XIXth Region by a secret door. The streets were deserted and calm. I ran with my pistol in my hand. At 26 Rue Michelet, Henri d'Astier de la Vigerie and José Aboulker were collating the information coming in from the different groups and following the course of the operation. They stayed near the radio, which was maintaining our liaison with the Allied fleet. They told me that Colonel Jousse was at police headquarters, so I went there and made my report. The colonel informed me that the message thrown out by General Koeltz was in our hands and that everything was proceeding according to plan.

Achiary, who was in a jovial mood, gave me some additional information. The occupation of police headquarters had gone well. A large part of the police thought it was a drill. The jails were full of the leaders of the SOL and the PPF; the DST brigade and a certain number of policemen had kept faith with Achiary. The post office, the prefecture, the police station, all of the objectives foreseen, were occupied. Mendigal was arrested, Juin was guarded closely by Bernard Pauphilet, as was Admiral Darlan, who had been passing through Algiers and happened to be with Juin at just the right moment.

I asked for two police inspectors to watch General Koeltz and 20 policemen to stand guard in front of the iron gate of the XIXth Region, so as to give a more official appearance to our enterprise. Finally, I returned with them to the XIXth Region and made my report to Pillafort.

A little after two in the morning, cannon shots, coming no doubt from the Admiralty, thundered in the night, proof that the Allied fleet was there. From Sidi-Ferruch to Fort-de-l'Eau the first commandos must have been landing.

Pillafort and I went to the Mogador center, where Pillafort told General Roubertie of the arrival of the Americans and the imminent arrival of Giraud. We had some coffee brought in, and Pillafort asked the general to join us, but he answered only that he would think about it. A few minutes later one of the guards brought in a message that Roubertie had been trying to pass secretly to the outside: "The American landing is only a trick. All available forces are ordered to put an end to this insurrection by every means possible."

General Koeltz, whom we went to see, was persisting in his attitude. "You will be shot!" he shouted on seeing us. Pointing to the two DST inspectors who were guarding him, he complained, "They dare to smoke in my presence!"

Indeed, Dominique Lentali, one of the veterans of Achiary's detachment, was sitting in the best armchair. He was short and rather plump, and his legs hardly touched the floor. At each puff, he sent the smoke in the general's direction, muttering, "I just can't stop myself from smoking!"

At three o'clock Pillafort sent me on a second mission to police headquarters, to inform them that we were certain that the 5th light infantry had been alerted and that we should expect a counterattack from its tanks very soon.

At police headquarters Achiary reported that the landing was under way. The cannon fire had been aimed at a destroyer trying to break through the barriers at the port. José Aboulker, who had just arrived, confirmed that the operation was taking place normally. General Mast and Colonel Jousse had just left for Staouéli to receive the first forces to land. They were to explain to them that our situation would become critical in a very short time, and to urge them to act quickly. In fact, Darlan had refused Murphy's request to give orders to prevent a useless battle, and Juin had followed his example.

Bob Murphy, so it appeared, was a little disoriented. The task was obviously delicate. To announce at midnight to Admiral Darlan, supreme commander of the French armed forces, and to General Juin, commander in chief in North Africa, that for the moment they were being "detained" at the Villa des Oliviers, and that Allied landings were in progress at Fedala, Port-Lyautey, Casablanca, Oran, and Algiers, was an undertaking that hardly resembled traditional diplomatic practice. When Darlan finally understood that, during those last few weeks, he had been royally taken in, he became so enraged that Murphy feared (so to speak) that he might collapse from a heart attack.

But the admiral was resourceful. He realized that only a trick would allow him to recover a certain room for maneuver, and, after having verified that he was indeed a prisoner, he pretended to calm down and asked Murphy for the authorization to send a personal letter to the Admiralty, giving his word of honor that the letter would contain no combat order. A member of the consulate took the letter to number 26, where Henri d'Astier asked him to read it. The letter contained formal orders to follow the armistice agreements and to resist the "aggressors" by every means possible.

A little later the admiral began his maneuver again with imperturbable composure, and again Robert Murphy took him at his word. This time the letter left for the Admiralty without passing through number 26; there was no suspicion about its contents.

At police headquarters, the policemen finally understood that this was not a simple drill. Some of them, along with their colleagues who had supported us from the beginning, expressed their joy and placed themselves at Achiary's disposal; others were less enthusiastic, but Raphaël, Fanfan,

Doctor Morali, and Daninos were firmly in control of the police substations.

José returned to warn us that Darlan's order, carried by an overconfident member of the United States consulate, had reached the Admiralty. There Major Dorange, General Juin's chief of staff, was calling out all of the forces he could get his hands on.

It was 4:30. With Achiary, José was busy keeping everything under control and trying to draw all the authorities who were asking for orders to police headquarters. There were already many people behind the bars of the underground cells. Some of them were glad to be relieved of all responsibility; others did not hide their fury.

I came back to the XIXth Region to make my report to Pillafort as dawn was breaking on Sunday, November 8. Up until 5:30 everything remained fairly calm. The number of prisoners grew rapidly. In spite of our proposals, none of them, at any time, agreed to join us. In the course of our rounds we stopped to see General Roubertie, calm and silent, and General Koeltz, still boiling over and furious, who called us "abominable profaners." I was astonished by his bizarre choice of words, but Pillafort said, in his calm and realistic tone, "Since we got him out of bed, Koeltz has been thinking only about his wounded vanity. Many of these generals, with their gold braid and honors, take themselves for living gods. They have such a high idea of themselves that even the defeat, in '40, of the armies that they commanded hasn't made them come down an inch from their pedestals. We have profaned the image that he had made of himself."

Day was about to break. We heard through the din of the navy cannons sounds of explosions and blasts that seemed to come from the city proper. Our own combat positions were reinforced, principally in the defense of the main gate, our most vulnerable point.

It was about 5:45. Pillafort, Daridan, and I were on the second floor of the XIXth Region when an alert rang through the building, shouted out by Lieutenant Jaïs, Libine, and Temime. Large units of the Mobile Guard had surrounded us and were preparing to attack.

"They are right on time," remarked Pillafort.

On the other side of the gate two noncommissioned officers, their assault rifles at their hips, their fingers on the triggers, aimed at us. Behind them were about 80 guards deployed in combat positions in the Rue Mogador, with several machine guns in place.

The colonel of the Mobile Guard approached; at his side were one of his officers and Major Dorange, in civilian clothes with a bullhorn in his hand. "Surrender immediately without conditions, or we open fire," he called to us.

Very calmly, without drawing his pistol, Pillafort spoke to them about the landing and the arrival of General Giraud.

"I am not here to argue; surrender immediately or I will open fire," the colonel replied.

"If you act this way, you're taking the side of the enemy who occupies our country. You are the authority for now, but in a few minutes our allies will be here and then you will be on the side of the traitors."

"You deserve 12 bullets in your skin and you shall have them."

"You too, shortly afterward."

Dorange intervened. His face like a knife blade was pale and stretched, but he was a calm man with his mind coldly made up. "Enough talk, colonel, we are wasting time. I order you in the name of the Marshal to do your duty. Attack."

Then, to Pillafort, "You're all going to get it. You've brought it on yourselves."

"I will at least have had time to express my scorn," Pillafort responded.

"I am doing my duty." He turned to the colonel. "I summon you to do yours."

The colonel repeated his order. "Last warning; surrender or I attack immediately."

"You will lose some feathers; we are well armed and entrenched," Pillafort answered calmly.

Edmond Benhamou approached Pillafort and, standing at attention, reported, "Captain, the machine guns are ready." We really had none.

"Listen, you are crazy; look at my position; we are higher than you on all sides; you will get yourselves killed to no purpose," said the colonel again.

Dorange was becoming impatient: "Colonel, once and for all, we are wasting time; let's finish this!"

"Look here, if you surrender, I will grant you the honors of war," said the colonel to Pillafort.

"For us, honor is not to surrender but to hold out until the Americans arrive. Every minute won means fewer dead."

"Let us have a *baroud* [an Arab word meaning combat] *d'honneur* and you surrender. Honor will be preserved on both sides."

"I think we do not have the same conception of *baroud* and honor."

"All right, I will attack and take your position."

"You will come in but first you will have to pass over my body."

The weapons of the two guards were pointed at us, their machine gun barrels less than 50 centimeters away. Beneath the helmets with straps stretched under the chin in German style, the expression on their faces was that of bulldogs awaiting the master's order. On our side were 50 men, determined and armed. Many of us would fall at the first volleys, but others were waiting in ambush behind windows or hidden in corners, ready to reply.

The reconquest of the XIXth Region was indispensable to organizing the operations against the landings effectively. Dorange was furious at the delay, and again he gave the colonel the order to "sweep us out of the way."

"Colonel, your name is Zwilling; you are Alsatian; think of Alsace," said Pillafort.

The colonel became somber. For the last few minutes he had been casting somewhat paternal glances at me.

"How old are you?"

If it were not a matter of gaining time, I would not have answered.

"Twenty."

The colonel turned to Pillafort: "Captain, you're leading a kid of 20 to his death?"

"Don't try that, it'll do no good," I said, to put an end to this intermission.

"So you all want to die?"

"After what I have been seeing for the last three years, if that continues any longer, I prefer to fall here. For that matter, you too, Colonel, are going to die; my men are not one-armed invalids," answered Pillafort.

Temime arrived, running.

"Captain, I've come from police headquarters. The Americans have penetrated into Algiers; they are in force; they will be here in half an hour."

The news was false, but it had its effect.

"Five hundred men at the utmost, who presently will be thrown back into the sea," said Dorange. "We know for an absolute fact that the Americans are not able to mount an operation of any size. It is Dieppe all over again."

No one budged on our side.

"You have thrown yourselves blindly into a foolish adventure," he continued. "You have committed an enormous mistake in wanting to help them. You will be shot."

Pillafort pointed out the fact that, for the moment, we were the ones holding prisoners, among them generals Koeltz and Roubertie. Dorange was concerned about the treatment we might have inflicted on them. Pillafort invited him and the colonel to pay them a visit.

"Give me your word of honor that you will let us come out again."

"You have it."

They agreed that the policemen, who had listened to this scene in silence, should withdraw. The gate was opened half way, and we took advantage of that to slip Daridan out to go and warn our comrades about our situation and to get information on the progress of the landings.

First we led Zwilling and Dorange to General Koeltz, who shouted, "They have dared to smoke in front of me. I want to leave immediately!"

"Yes, General," said Zwilling.

"With my car and chauffeur."

"Yes, General.

"And with my colors."

"With the colors, General."

"Destroy these buildings and all they contain with your cannon, immediately. They have been profaned!"

At that point, Zwilling remained silent. As for us, it was a matter of occupying the XIXth Region as long as possible, to continue to paralyze the Mogador center. The only way was to make the discussion last, and we felt that, tacitly, Zwilling was in agreement about temporizing. We obtained an hour's delay before the attack if we freed the two generals, and after some new discussion we agreed to liberate all the prisoners on condition that the hour would begin to be counted only after the last prisoner had left. The two generals left first, then little by little the others. Naturally we dragged out each departure to the maximum extent.

But the tension increased. A new compromise: at the end of the elapsed hour the attack would be delayed again on condition that our troops evacuate the XIXth Region. Pillafort, Libine, and I alone would remain to occupy it.

Then we saw Daridan approaching the iron grill: "Giraud has just spoken on the radio; he is taking command of all the troops in North Africa."

Pillafort advised Zwilling to put himself under the orders of General Giraud. Dorange had suddenly disappeared.

"After all, I am an Alsatian. I don't like the Boche. I hereby end hostilities against you," Zwilling finally declared.

We lifted Pillafort into the air and sang the *Marseillaise*.

Three light tanks of the 5th infantry had come to take up positions on Bugeaud Square at about 30 meters from the gate. They pointed their 37-caliber cannons at us, and a major alighted from the nearest tank. Zwilling agreed that Pillafort should try to engage in a dialogue with them, and I went with him; Libine took up a position midway to maintain the liaison with our comrades, who had returned to their combat positions. We would be allowed to go back into the XIXth Region whatever the outcome of the parley.

This major wore the helmet of the tank troops; his face was all stitched with scars. He was an old veteran who knew Pillafort.

"Well, so it's you. You're behaving like a street ruffian," he called out.

"I have no choice. Where are the Americans?"

"Haven't seen any. You've gotten yourself into a dirty mess. I should shoot you down."

"Go ahead if you want to; for me it's 12 bullets in my hide or victory today."

Daridan came up and repeated Giraud's radio declaration. He affirmed that he had observed the reality and the size of the American landing.

The tension was eased. We all understood that it was no longer a time for shooting one another, and we agreed that everyone should simply withdraw. We returned to the courtyard of the XIXth Region and had the weapons stacked. Pillafort instructed our group to rest for a while and then to regroup in two hours at the Salle Géo Gras.

The tanks and the Mobile Guards had withdrawn and we were left alone, Pillafort, Daridan, Libine, Jaïs, Temime, Benhamou, and I. The XIXth Region was completely empty, the Mogador center deprived of its personnel and out of service. It was nine in the morning; the game seemed to have been won.

We had three autos at our disposal, and at my suggestion we decided to get something to eat at my parents' house at Mont-Hydra. From the heights of Algiers we would have a better idea of the extent of the landing. From the Rue Michelet, as far up as Galand Park, there was a panoramic view of the port and the bay. The enormous armada was there. We had been expecting it, we had entertained no doubts, and yet we could hardly believe our eyes. The great gray ships filled the bay, cruisers, torpedo boats, an innumerable quantity of troop transports. The cannons of the Admiralty were still thundering but the reality of it overwhelmed us with joy.

We stopped at Poulet's villa to tell her that all was well. She was happy, very much moved. The gendarmes at the Voirol Column watched us pass. Temime shouted to them, "They got it in the ass, those Germans!" They didn't know what to think.

At Mont-Hydra, anxiety gave way to profound joy. While food was being prepared, we talked in the smoking room with my father. He was planning to put his entire property at the disposal of General Giraud, to help him in his first difficulties. "When we heard the cannon," he said, "we understood that it was the real thing and that you were lucky."

My little brother, Lionel, who was 12, was there too, very much interested. We sat down to table and, in a few minutes, gobbled up fried eggs once over, washed down with wine from our farm. Then we climbed back into the cars to go down to police headquarters on the Boulevard Baudin.

At the Voirol Column the road was blockaded by two wagons loaded with bales of hay. Five helmeted gendarmes, armed with muskets, were waiting for us there. Pillafort, Libine, and I in the first car smashed through; the second car, with Daridan and Jaïs, got through, too; but the gendarmes opened fire on the third, where Edmond Benhamou and Temime were. We backed up and got out. Benhamou and Temime were not wounded, but the gendarmes announced that we were under arrest. Pillafort quickly explained the situation to them and asked for the right to pass, but they refused and ordered us to follow them to the gendarmerie. We took out our revolvers and warned them to let us alone. Benhamou left us, to notify police headquarters.

While we were arguing, an automobile had come up to the barrier. It appeared suspicious to us, and we stopped it. Inside were officers who, not knowing who we were, announced that they were going "into the interior to organize resistance to the landing." We took them prisoner.

The Voirol Column happened to be the departure point from Algiers toward the south. From now on, judging it important for us to stay right there, and ignoring the sporadic protests of the gendarmes, we began to stop all cars and seize all those who might interfere with the landing. In a few minutes we had captured about 20 autos containing about 40 officers, among them several colonels and an admiral, as well as one car containing Admiral Darlan's luggage.

The secretary general of the prefecture, Louis Périllier, presented himself at our barrier; he was a friend of my father, and we were aware of his pro-Allies sentiments. Pillafort wrote out a pass for him.

The cannon thundered unceasingly in the bay. A few shells landed nearby on the edge of the Bois de Boulogne, and a few curious people who had gone there were wounded. I caught sight of Denise and her father, come to see what was going on. Expelled from Alsace in 1940, they now lived in Hydra. I told them about the landing and advised them to return home. They left in a happy frame of mind. My brother Gérard joined us and helped for a moment, but I asked him to think of my parents' anxiety and to go to reassure them.

Benhamou returned accompanied by José Aboulker, Bernard Karsenty, and three other comrades. José was carrying the submachine gun that Murphy had given him, the only one of all those that we were supposed to receive. Bernard carried an automatic carbine, a present from General Clark. They brought about a dozen policemen as reinforcements, and we arrested the gendarmes; leaving the policemen with the responsibility of stopping incoming vehicles, we went on toward police headquarters, some of us leading the cars we had stopped, with their occupants, and the others guarding the rear of the procession. It was eleven in the morning when we arrived at police headquarters. Our prisoners were put into the jail, while José and Bernard gave us the latest information.

Darlan had been freed at five o'clock by Dorange and the Mobile Guard. From Fort l'Empereur, a bastion dating from the time of the corsairs which overlooks the bay, he was trying to direct the operations. The Mobile Guard, the 5th infantry, the 13th Senegalese, the navy, and the navy gendarmerie had little by little retaken the posts held by the VP. It was Raphaël who had read over the radio the declaration by General Giraud, of whom we had no news. General de Monsabert had waited all night at Blida for the arrival of the airplane; he was now in an unpleasant situation, facing troops brought from the Joinville air base, which had been alerted from Fort l'Empereur, where General Juin, too, had installed himself.

Many of our comrades had been taken prisoner by the Mobile Guard, at the Winter Palace and at the Pélissier barracks, and by the sailors of the Admiralty at the residences of General Juin and General Mendigal. The prefecture had been evacuated without any losses and with the weapons. At the main post office, which Lieutenant Jean Dreyfus was holding, elements of the 5th infantry had opened fire, and it appeared that Dreyfus had been killed. Some SOL opened fire with a machine gun on the group that was holding the telephone center. Our comrades returned fire, and one of the SOL was brought down, but the others fled. The groups that had tried to occupy the Admiralty had been taken prisoner.

Colonel Jousse was able to make contact with the first American elements to land at Sidi-Ferruch. He kept urging their leader, General Ryder, to accelerate the occupation of Algiers, which was moving rather slowly. He managed to get an American detachment to relieve General de Monsabert at Blida.

In the bay the cannon continued to thunder. The Allied warships that tried to penetrate into the harbor received serious damage. One of them succeeded in landing a commando unit, which was now blocked on the Agha quay, from which thick smoke was rising. A big three-stack troopship broke through the barricade at the harbor entrance; it drove through with its enormous mass and with all the force of its engines, stopped finally by a collision with the railroad pier. Troops were landing under fire from the Admiralty.

Police headquarters was the only strategic point that we still held and, except for the harbor, the Americans had not moved in from the outskirts of Algiers. Nevertheless, it was too late for the Vichy forces to be able to organize an effective opposition to the landing. By completely paralyzing them until five in the morning, our attempt had succeeded far better than we could have hoped. Meanwhile fighting was taking place from Fort-de-l'Eau to Sidi-Ferruch, and we had at all costs to prevent the arrival of reinforcements to oppose the Allies.

Pillafort sent Benhamou and Morali to rouse up our friends at the Salle Géo Gras. Other groups joined us, and soon we numbered more than a hundred men, of whom many were policemen. The Boulevard Baudin was practically the only way to cross Algiers to send troops toward the east and west, and we quickly set up a barricade blocking traffic. We seized two motorized 75 assault cannons that were speeding toward Fort-de-l'Eau. Placed in firing position on both sides of the headquarters, they created between them a space of about a hundred meters, which served as a trap and an entrenchment.

Some SOL had occupied the balconies of the upper floors of the buildings opposite the headquarters. They shot at us steadily but, lying on their stomachs behind the balconies, they did not even show their heads and could not adjust their range; the noise of their firing was hardly audible in the rumble of the cannonade. From time to time a bullet flattened itself on the pavement at our feet. We did not reply.

Some of the policemen noticed that I had only a 6.35. I had not thought of keeping any of the larger caliber weapons that I had seized. They took me to a cellar, where hundreds of prisoners were crammed together in the jails. On one of the tables were hundreds of weapons. I chose a nine-shot 7.65.

We stopped many vehicles loaded with troops, munitions, shells, mortars, machine guns. The officers were stuffed into the jails. Not one agreed to join us. The halls of police headquarters were soon full to overflowing, and the newest arrivals were shut up in the corridors of adjacent buildings.

Henri d'Astier, José, and Bernard Karsenty went back and forth between the Boulevard Baudin and 26 Rue Michelet, keeping us informed of the progress of the Americans, who were beginning to move into the city.

We intercepted several ambulances, which we inspected and immediately let go on their way to the Maillot Hospital. Most of the wounded were Senegalese; some were already dead. In one ambulance there were wounded Americans, the first I had seen.

At about two in the afternoon Pillafort and I had just stopped a truck loaded with cases of ammunition. While we were handing it over to the policemen, we saw a military vehicle coming, heading toward Hussein-dey. We approached it. Pillafort was negligently holding his revolver by the trigger guard. When he reached the car, he signaled it to put on its brakes. In a flash, I saw the left rear door open slightly; the barrel of a pistol appeared and was fired at him. Several bullets whistled past my head. Inside the auto, in the right rear seat was a colonel; to the left, a major; in front on the left, a captain; on the right, the chauffeur. Pillafort fired and so did I. Shots rang out on all sides. I emptied my magazine; Pillafort was reloading his weapon. The major had sunk down in his seat; the captain was protecting himself under the instrument panel; the driver, his eyes wild, got out of the vehicle. The colonel let his weapon fall; he tried to open the door on the right side, half opened it, and leaned outside. His helmet fell to the ground. A policeman moved around the car and shot point blank into the colonel's skull. Blood gushed out. From the balconies, the SOL fired on us steadily, and a strafing of machine-gun fire transformed the auto into a holocaust.

Pillafort was leaning against a pillar of the arcade; I went over to him. "They got me," he said.

Fired at close range, the bullet from the Colt had hit him in the right side of his stomach. José Aboulker, a doctor, arrived and examined the wound. "It's serious," he said.

While he looked for an ambulance, we carried Pillafort into a room at police headquarters and stretched him out on a table. When I asked to stay with him, he told me to go back to the Boulevard Baudin to continue directing the action there. The ambulance arrived, and Pillafort was put into it. From his stretcher he instructed me to hold out as long as possible, and to come to see him at the Solal Clinic after the operation.

The captures continued, among them several trucks loaded with marines going toward Hussein-dey. At about 3:30, I saw Colonel Zwilling, alone and on foot. He recognized me and came toward us.

"I commend you for this morning. How far have you gotten?"

I explained things to him and asked him if he would agree to take charge of the action.

"Very well, I'll be back," and he went off toward the Rue Charras.

We noticed a change among the policemen. Some of their leaders who had supported Achiary were impressed by the fusillade a moment ago. Furthermore, we had promised them the Americans at two in the morning, and it was now four in the afternoon. Some of the policemen who had been put in jail were released, and one of them came to me to reclaim the weapon that I had picked up from the table. I gave it back to him and took my 6.35 out of my pocket again.

At about 4:30, more vehicles loaded with marines tried to break through the barricade. We stopped them, but the officer who was sitting with his men in the back of one of the trucks aimed his pistol at me when I ordered him to get down. Insanely, he pulled the trigger. I heard the click of the pin, but the shot did not go off. Then he let his weapon fall into my out-stretched hand, and the others handed over their muskets.

Some of the policemen called to me, "You're wanted downstairs in headquarters."

"Don't go!" Germain Libine shouted.

He was right. They were policemen who had just been released and who were trying to draw me toward the jail. I aimed at them and they disap-peared.

A bullet landed at my feet, shot from the balconies. I seized a rifle from one of the piles of weapons heaped up on the sidewalk, cocked it, and raised it to my shoulder. Daridan turned the barrel aside and looked at me with his sky-blue eyes. I uncocked the rifle and cast it aside.

Toward five, Bernard Karsenty came back from number 26 to inform us that a cease-fire had been declared. The Americans were now occupying the suburbs. The cannons were still thundering, but for a few minutes no vehicles had come to throw themselves into our trap. Zwilling had not come back. Our action was over. We decided to withdraw, arranging to meet again the next morning at number 26.

Following the Rue Michelet, I went up to the Solal Clinic, where some-one told me how to find room 33. Pillafort had just undergone an opera-tion. When he woke up and asked me about our progress, I told him that a cease-fire had been declared and that the Americans were investing the city. We had won. He asked me to go to tell Poulet that he was wounded, so I left on foot for the heights of Algiers.

In front of the Summer Palace I met the first American commandos, who had just captured the German consul and were threatening him. As I drew near Sainte-Marie church I heard detonations. A young American officer had just been shot and his comrades were standing around him; he was breathing his last as I came abreast of him. One of the few passers-by informed me that it was a lieutenant of the 5th infantry who had shot him in the back and then fled up the stairs of the Chemin de Gascogne.

Poulet gathered some things and we went down to the clinic on a trolley bus that was running again. In his white room on the fourth floor Pillafort was in great pain. He said that he had already been wounded in the stom-ach in Morocco, that it was nothing; in three weeks we would drink champagne together to celebrate our success and his cure. Poulet stayed behind to help the nurses.

I found a trolley bus going up toward Hydra. Night had come. At the Voirol Column Allied vehicles were positioned on the square. They had arrived. I told my parents briefly what had transpired since the morning; I ate something and then went up to my room, where I put a Hersthal 7.65 that I had taken from a colonel, as well as a Rubis 7.65 taken from a marine, into a drawer; and I put my 6.35 under my pillow.

My father joined me in my room. "You shot at those officers? It's not possible."

"Yes, I did."

"How could you?"

"They were firing at Pillafort; they were firing at me."

"If the SOL come here tonight, or the Mobile Guard, jump out the window: I will detain them as long as necessary."

"Don't worry. They have better things to do."

He kissed me. My father, who had raised me saying, "Only art is great." I got into bed; bells and drums rang in my head. I went to sleep.

The next morning before eight I went down to the clinic. The trolley buses had resumed their normal routine, and Algiers was now solidly held by the Allies. Many of the soldiers were English, recognizable from their battle dress, but they wore on their left sleeve a little American flag so as to be taken for Americans.

At the clinic I found Poulet again, and Professor Solal. Pillafort had survived the operation but the wound was very serious. Perforation of the liver and intestines. The bullet had lodged next to the spinal column and they had not been able to extract it. In a voice that he tried to make cheerful, he asked me to go for news from number 26 and to come back later in the morning. Daridan arrived and we went together to number 26.

The Aboulkers' apartment was in a state of siege. The SOL had not disarmed, and reprisal raids were feared. But it was well guarded, principally by groups from the Salle Géo Gras. The Americans had given us two machine guns.

Dreyfus had been killed. Yesterday at eight he had been shot down by a volley in the back fired by an adjutant of the 5th infantry when, after parleys, he was returning to the main post office to have it evacuated by his men. There were a few wounded, but very slightly, by the firing of the SOL. Monsabert had been relieved. There was no news of the Admiralty group; it appeared that they were all prisoners, and we feared some might have been killed. Henri d'Astier, José Aboulker, and Bernard Karsenty were trying to get Murphy to force the navy to make an accounting.

The French battleships and submarines based at Algiers, the guns of the Admiralty, the marines, the Senegalese, the few troops that were alerted in spite of everything, had caused damage to the Allied ships and troops, but nothing compared to what we had feared.

We could now judge the extraordinary success of our action. In the morning it had not been possible for the Vichy command to effectively take control of what means they had at their disposal. Up to the cease-fire we had disorganized their liaisons, stopped most of the officers who tried to transmit combat orders, prevented large numbers of troops from opposing the Allies, and seized an enormous amount of heavy and light weapons and munitions. Our action had certainly saved thousands of human lives, wrecked the Vichy plan for cobelligerence with the Axis, and brought France back into the camp of the Allies before it was too late.

It appeared that at Oran and Casablanca, where those who were supposed to act as we did had been neutralized almost immediately, the battle was now raging furiously. The rapid success at Algiers, the most important objective, would guarantee the success of all the others. We were aware of the immense turnaround of the war in 24 hours. After their demoralizing experiences in the Pacific, the Americans had successfully carried off their first operation in the West. It was the beginning of the reconquest.

Through the windows we could see the jeeps and the G.M.C.'s passing, often driven by young Hebrews. It was a small revenge on the inhabitants of the Rue Michelet who, from behind their curtains, were watching the troop movements.

We were still waiting for General Giraud. In the confusion that reigned we could not learn the reasons for his delay. It was of the greatest importance that, as soon as possible, Giraud should assume the functions of civil and military leader that had been guaranteed to him by the agreements with Roosevelt and Murphy.

When I returned to Mont-Hydra for lunch, Guédri, our chauffeur, was there. With three other Kabyles who were not then assigned, he had been sent to reinforce the group at the Admiralty. At dawn things had taken a turn for the worse; the marines had surrounded them and had fired warning shots. Taking advantage of the dark, Guédri and his Kabyles had managed to slip away; the marines had taken them for fishermen, unable to imagine for a moment that Moslems, those brainless shadows that were part of the decoration, could take part in such an action. But all the others were prisoners. Principally concerned was the Hydra-Mustaphy group directed by Reserve Lieutenant André Cohen. Among them were André Rosfelder, Jean Snyers, Jean Mazel, David Cohen, the Hartwig brothers, and Jean and Roland Faugère.

In the afternoon Pillafort, whose condition seemed satisfactory, explained to me that his hope was to form all of us into a commando unit which, as soon as possible, would fight against the Germans. I talked about it with Pauphilet and with a few other comrades. We were enthusiastic.

In the evening Benhamou and Roger Morali, fearing something might happen to my parents, insisted on coming to spend the night with me at Mont-Hydra. Information received pointed to the possibility of SOL raids, and our villa was isolated. The next morning I went back and forth between the clinic and 26 Rue Michelet, where our permanent command post was situated.

We watched the funeral procession of Colonel Jacquin pass by. That was the name of the man whose violent resistance to the landing led him to that crazy act on the Boulevard Baudin. He had been in command of the antiaircraft batteries. Furious that his cannons, his machine guns, and his men had been taken from him, he had come to reconnoiter on the Rue Charras and had said, "We will shoot the leader; the others will run like a flock of sparrows." I could see again his insane eyes when he shot Pillafort. The hearse was buried in flowers, and all the authorities were there.

Giraud was delayed at Gibraltar. The Americans did not want to be embarrassed in their negotiations with Darlan, who even though he had accepted a cease-fire for the region of Algiers, where the game was up for him, was allowing the Germano-Vichy plan of defense to be pursued everywhere else and continuing to affirm his loyalty to Pétain and Laval.

Severe battles were in progress at Oran, Casablanca, Port-Lyautey, Fedala. We knew from the United States consulate that Admiral Platon had been sent to Tunis by Vichy to order Admiral Estéva, the resident general, and Admiral Derrien, the maritime prefect, to give aid to the Germans, who were beginning to occupy Tunisia without being subjected to a single gunshot.

Here, we were still unaware of the fate of our comrades at the Admiralty. We knew that the SOL were getting organized and were preparing reprisals of all kinds.

At the end of the morning we went up to the Jewish cemetery to bury Dreyfus in the utmost simplicity. Under the blue sky, the rabbi read a short prayer while the coffin was lowered into the grave. The father and mother stood straight, dignified. From the rest, not a word, not a comment.

In the afternoon our liaison with the United States consulate informed us that Darlan, supported less and less by his officers, had made up his mind to order a cease-fire for all of North Africa. General Juin intervened in this regard in the most urgent way. Meanwhile the admiral had exhausted all of his means of resisting the Allied landing. In the afternoon of November 8, he had received through the Admiralty an encoded telegram containing the proposal of the OKW, Hitler's combined interservice general staff, to send the Axis planes based in Sicily to oppose the landings. This secret dispatch requested precise information on the priority of the objectives to be attacked. Immediately, Darlan had specified, "The transports at sea off Algiers." It was in Algiers that, as a result of our action, Darlan found himself in a most critical situation, and that was where he wanted to be relieved first of all, knowing that the Allied successes in Algiers signified the eventual success of the landings at Oran and in Morocco. If he specified, "At sea off Algiers," it was, without any doubt, so that the Vichy units that were still fighting around the city would not be demoralized by the spectacle of the Luftwaffe coming to their aid. The raid by the Axis planes had, in fact, taken place, causing significant losses to the Allied transports.

We were making some progress in our own affairs. André Achiary, on his own authority, resumed his position as head of the Direction of Security of the Territory. With his inspectors he set himself up on the Rue Denfert-Rochereau in the offices of the Italian House, formerly a meeting place for Axis spies. Bernard Pauphilet and Jean Arguillère, with their group, had occupied the offices of the PPF at 7 Rue Charras. We decided to make it the headquarters of our future commando group.

At the clinic, Pillafort's condition seemed better, and I kept him informed about everything. The coming of General Giraud and the respecting of the agreements by the Americans were the questions that preoccupied him the most. In the evening we witnessed the first evening air raid on the city, the harbor, the boats in the bay. The Allied antiaircraft fire had a power that we had not imagined. The damage was of little importance; several planes fell into the sea in flames.

For the night we installed ourselves defensively at number 26. Whether the information was valid or not, it might now be the objective of the SOL. But nothing happened except that, because of a false alert, Benhamou slipped in the hall and sprayed us with a volley from his machine gun. Luckily only one person was wounded, Guy Cohen, in his ankle.

On November 11 we learned that Giraud had finally arrived, but he was quarantined and without power at Lemaigre-Dubreuil's Villa Mahieddine. Henri d'Astier had just come back from there, very much disturbed. Giraud, who had learned at Gibraltar that General Eisenhower had been designated as the only Allied commander, in absolute contradiction to the duly signed accords, had almost refused to go to Algiers; then, learning at Dar Mahieddine what was going on in the city, he was on the verge of leaving again. Lemaigre-Dubreuil, who was the principal artisan of Giraud's arrival, was crushed by the news.

"Courage, General, be resolute! We thought we were installing an eagle in Algiers and your attitude is that of a sparrow," he had declared.

Henri d'Astier had finally found a convincing argument: "Your appeal to the army of Africa and to all Frenchmen was broadcast on the morning of November 8, over the frequencies of Radio Algiers, as though it was you reading it. You would be the laughing stock of the universe if you left today."

Giraud had agreed to remain, but he was taking no action. In the confusion, the case containing his uniform and his képi with oak leaves had been lost at Blida on the night of November 7, and he would not even consider showing himself in civilian clothes; he would, as he saw it, be quite naked without the authority of his stars. A tailor had been sent to the Villa Mahieddine to put together a new uniform.

Toward eleven, Raphaël, Fanfan, and I went from the clinic to the Mustapha Hospital to get the equipment for an oxygen tent. Pillafort was beginning to have pulmonary complications, but the doctors did not seem worried.

At noon I returned to number 26; Henri d'Astier was there, upset. The Americans had just signed some accords with Darlan, accords of the victors over the vanquished. Darlan had made every concession in order to remain in power. The Giraud-Murphy agreements — according to which France was considered to be the equal of the English and the Americans, the integrity of all our territories was guaranteed, the supreme command of all Allied forces was to be held by General Giraud as long as the Anglo-American troops were not superior in number to the French troops in North Africa — were now being scorned. In place of a government of liberation, free and independent, directed by an unquestioned leader, the Americans had installed a gauleiter submitting to all their demands; they knew that Darlan had already, in dealing with the Germans, shown a flexibility that had led him to treason.

To reach this point, it had taken three days of fighting, in which the French lost 3,000 men and the Allies almost as many. The naval losses were particularly high on both sides. We stupidly lost most of our warships and submarines based in North Africa, when they could have been assigned to guard the coast of Tunisia, where Admiral Estéva was doing all he could to assist the arrival of the Germans. Giraud was disoriented, without power, with no support but ours, and we could do nothing. But everything was not negative. General Juin had offered General Giraud his own place as commander in chief in North Africa and had ordered General Barré, commander of the troops in Tunisia, to regroup his forces so as to be in a position to block the Germans as soon as possible.

Finally, Murphy had an injunction sent to the Admiralty. If the sailors did not immediately free our comrades, they would be bombarded by the American air forces. But no reply had come so far. Entrenched in their white fortress on the peninsula opposite the city, the sailors were burning their archives.

We were in complete confusion. One fact was certain: nothing was happening as we had imagined it. That the Americans should break their agreements, that General Clark, the man on the submarine, should have broken his word, that Darlan should be in power while Allied troops tranquilly crisscrossed the city, all that was unimaginable for us.

We decided to alert all of the groups to be ready for any eventuality. I went with Germain Libine to the Salle Géo Gras, where more than 200 of our comrades were meeting. We tempered their bitterness somewhat. Nothing was definite yet; a few hours from now, relieved of their first cares, Murphy and Eisenhower would surely honor their engagements. But it was obvious that we were isolated, and we laid out a plan for communication centers in order to have a contingent ready at all times. In any case, everyone considered himself to be mobilized. Since November 7 not one of us had been separated from his weapon. But what else could we do now but defend ourselves? A Trojan horse is good only once.

When we went out on Government Square, it was night, but the sky was illuminated by the antiaircraft tracer shells in a display of fireworks encircling the bay. From time to time there was a great flame in the black sky; it was a bomber exploding. Algiers was now on the right side of the war under the protection of the Allied guns. What did people think about it? They were taking things as they came, wondering, and expecting solemn but glorious times.

I went back to the clinic. Pillafort's hoarse voice worried me. They were afraid that the many internal perforations had reopened. Poulet reported that in the afternoon policemen had come and had started in to interrogate Pillafort concerning the circumstances of the fusillade in the Boulevard Baudin. He replied that he alone had answered the shooting started by the occupants of the car. When Poulet interfered, to make them let him alone, the policemen became rude. Seizing Poulet, they tried to drag her out, and Pillafort then started to get up to defend her. Some doctors entered, and the policemen left, but it was feared that some stitches might have been pulled out.

And we had not organized a guard during the day! He had not been willing. But we had not been imagining things. As soon as he was notified of the incident, José got the United States consulate to send American soldiers to mount guard in front of the door of his room.

As much as possible, we announced only good news to Pillafort, but now he knew that the Americans were making a deal with Darlan, that all of the Vichy authorities had remained in place, and that Giraud was being courted. When I told him that everything would come out right, he only answered me, "My dear Mario. . . ."

The Janons came in, and we surrounded our friend with all our immense affection; that might do him the most good. Then we let him rest. Only Poulet remained.

At Mont-Hydra, Bernard Giraud came to pay a visit to my father. He was one of the general's sons and a friend of my brother. My father spoke with him about Pillafort and Dreyfus and his admiration for them. The telephone rang: it was André Rosfelder, who had been freed and was now home with his parents. He and his comrades spent four days in the underground dungeons of the Admiralty. The navy kept announcing that they would be executed, and twice the naval officers made them go to the courtyard and lined them up against the wall before a squad of Senegalese; but in the end they didn't dare.

"We were taken prisoner because we were not morally prepared for Frenchmen to shoot each other. They were," André told us.

The radio announced the invasion of the Free Zone by the Germans.

The next morning Pillafort's condition was described by the doctors as stable, but I found him to be more weary. Although he said nothing about it, the intrusion by the policemen had given him a severe setback. Two Americans were on guard in front of his door.

At number 26 the atmosphere was heavy. For the moment, General Clark was leaving all civilian and military authorities in place. Those of us who were in touch with the American consulate felt ourselves becoming annoyances, encumbrances. We had the feeling that, now we had accomplished our task, we were in the way. The American generals had no desire to share their first success of the war with a group of partisans. General Mast, Colonel Jousse, Captain Bouin, and Lieutenant Daridan were dismissed. Clark and Murphy had even granted Juin's request that they not be allowed to wear their uniforms. Darlan held all civilian and military powers and claimed that he alone could rally the French fleet immobilized at Toulon by the armistice accords. We recognized that this possibility was important enough to justify patience. Doubtless he would attempt to bring about this recovery of the fleet in order to secure a major trump card that would help to maintain him in power.

As of the day before, I had taken my group in hand. Number 7 Rue Charras, the former headquarters of the PPF, was under permanent guard. We had found some friends among the English. Having taken the largest part in the landings and suffered the most losses, the British, too, felt cheated by the Americans, who had changed the original plans and were now behaving like the only victors, making all the decisions. Pauphilet and Arguillère obtained from British headquarters the tacit recognition of our organization, which was assuming the name of the "French Commando." At the Rue Charras we spent the day storing arms, munitions, and equipment. We now had many Sten machine guns, and we gave a few of them to number 26, others to Achiary. Faces were getting brighter; we were no longer alone.

At the end of the afternoon Pauphilet and I went to the clinic to tell Pillafort about the formation of the French Commando. Soon he would be the one to give the final touches to the preparation for our departure toward Tunisia, where fighting was expected. He would have under his orders several hundred volunteers who had the greatest admiration for him.

That evening at Mont-Hydra my father told me that he had had a half-hour conversation with General Giraud that afternoon. He had reminded him of our action, which had made possible his arrival, and of the sacrifice of Dreyfus.

"Pillafort is seriously wounded. For you."

"I know."

"Pillafort is a hero."

"Yes, a hero."

"Will you not go and give him the comfort of your presence?"

"I will go."

My father had informed him that he was putting at his disposal all of his possessions, to help in raising troops. Giraud thanked him: "But there is no need; I have just signed an order of general mobilization."

"Thousands of people are detained in unspeakable conditions in the internment camps of Boghar, Berrouaghia, Adjerat M'Ghil, Bossuet, Méchéria, for political or racial motives. They must be liberated without delay."

"I will see about it."

Our telephone rang. It was Professor Jahier, who wanted to tell us how much Pillafort's condition was worrying him. The next morning, November 13, Pillafort's condition deteriorated. He was breathing with difficulty, his temperature had risen still more; his weak, hollow voice was heartbreaking. José Aboulker was beside him, somber and troubled. Poulet arrived; she had taken a few hours' rest. We spoke softly.

All day long at the Rue Charras we were busy solving the problems of the commando. For the moment this command post was adequate for us; it was vast, including several halls, offices, and also store rooms that filled the entire basement of the building. But we would need a training camp with housing for the recruits, a food supply, vehicles; and furthermore, since Giraud was going to order a general mobilization, our situation had to be regularized with respect to the French authorities, so that we might accept enlistments according to proper procedure, beginning with our own, so as not to be considered deserters by our original military corps. Meanwhile we registered provisional enlistments and drew up lists of our effectives; we organized the functioning of our base and expanded our contacts with the British in order to obtain what we lacked. Bernard Pauphilet and Arguillère were the administrators, making the major decisions. Kiko, André Rosfelder, Thoumazeau, Marcel Fellus, Sirot, Temime, Pierre Chesnais, Henri Mesguich, other comrades, devoted all of their time to the commando and left the premises only to sleep.

As evening fell, Germain Libine came to join me and we went to the clinic. Poulet, Madame Janon, Raphaël, and Professor Solal were there. They seemed to be reassured. "The worst days are over," they said. "He has survived the crucial period; he's going to make it."

Germain and I threw our arms around each other. I drew near the bed. Pillafort took my hand and slowly raised it to his lips.

On November 14, at eight in the morning, I got off the trolley bus near the clinic. Daridan's son was waiting for me, and he took my arm. "He is dead," he said.

In the empty room Pillafort was at rest. The expression on his face was triumphant. For a moment I remained alone with my friend. For me everything had crumbled. Slowly, as if in a trance, I went down toward number 26. Pain and consternation reigned there. The friend, the respected companion in our struggles was no more; he had been so strong that he had seemed indestructible.

Bitterness was added to our sorrow. Clark officially confirmed that all civilian and military authorities were to be maintained in their posts under the control of Darlan. This time it was no longer an expedient justified by urgency; the decision was deliberate, heavy with consequences.

Henri d'Astier was there, doubly stricken by Pillafort's death and the turn of events. He was overwhelmed, a man who habitually seemed so reserved, almost enigmatic, and who hid the warmth of his feelings under an apparent self-possession. He informed me that, among the Group of Five, some, making the best of the situation, were ready to collaborate with Darlan, provided they were assigned to important posts.

Once again, we could weigh the extent of the disaster caused by Darlan's presence in Algiers. If Juin had been reconfirmed in his command, as early as the morning of November 8 he would have given the cease-fire order to the troops of North Africa. Giraud would not have been held back at Gibraltar and his accords with Murphy flouted. But the Americans at Oran and in Morocco had faced much stronger opposition than anticipated; after that, they could not resist the temptation to make advantageous agreements, even if it meant going back on their previous engagements. We thought bitterly that, if Darlan had not been there, Pillafort would certainly not have died, since the barricade in the Boulevard Baudin would not have been needed.

Daridan was with us. The very strong friendship that united us was a comfort to us, but we knew that for both of us, apart from our grief, nothing worse could have happened. With Pillafort, everything had been simple and wonderful. Now we were alone to face all that lay ahead.

The next day we were still unable to obtain a burial permit. The government officials were waiting for orders. Some were timorous; others had recovered their arrogance. As of the day before, Darlan was officially the high commissioner for North Africa, with General Noguès, General Bergeret, and Governor Chatel, the leading Vichy chiefs who were in their posts before the landing, to be his principal adjuncts. Giraud had agreed to place himself under Darlan's orders; he was named commander in chief of the troops. These measures were proclaimed "in the name of the Marshal, who was unable to be present."

On the morning of the sixteenth, Pillafort was placed in a coffin and transported to the depository on Villaret de Joyeuse Avenue. We covered the coffin with a tricolor flag on which we put his uniform jacket. There were a few of us, Poulet, the Janons, the Daridans, Henri d'Astier and Madame d'Astier, Cordier, Mesguich, Germain Libine, and other comrades, who were waiting for the body to be moved.

Twelve English soldiers commanded by Bob, an English officer who was a friend of ours, presented arms when the coffin was lifted onto the hearse. We would meet at the Saint-Augustin church, where the religious ceremony was to take place. Pierre-Marie Cordier and I sat side by side in the tram, but we spoke very little. I noticed that he was praying discreetly, and he saw that I had noticed.

"Did you know I am a priest?"

"No, I didn't know that."

Now I could understand his simplicity, his modesty, his clothing of very ordinary material totally lacking in style; his appearance had made me think of a character out of Dostoevski.

In front of the Saint-Augustin church a crowd of our friends was assembled. Large police contingents surrounded us, perhaps to protect us, since the threats of the SOL were not forgotten; doubtless also to show us that we were barely tolerated, even in circumstances when enmity would normally be suspended.

Bernard Pauphilet and other comrades of the Rue Charras had come in two autos from which the barrels of two Sten guns quite visibly protruded. The police chief in full dress uniform came over toward me. "What are your intentions?"

"To bury our captain, in peace if possible."

My father was there; the church was filled with those whom a communion of ideas, of struggles, of sorrows, of hopes, brought together. Giraud was absent. He had not appeared in any way whatever.

The funeral service was over; as soon as the coffin was again on the hearse, the police chief gave the chauffeur a signal and he took off at full speed toward the Saint-Eugène cemetery. The police formed a barricade to prevent us from following, but we immediately rushed them; some of us ran; others jumped on a moving tram; my father, Cordier, and I climbed into a carriage passing by. We arrived at the entrance to the cemetery at the same time as the hearse.

The grave had been dug on the hillside among the cypress trees, near the basilica of Notre-Dame d'Afrique.

Bonnier
de la Chapelle

$\mathcal{I}$N SPITE OF THE CONFUSION AROUND US, we were getting organized at the Rue Charras. Our aim was to meet the Germans in Tunisia, where they were establishing themselves in full force, as quickly as possible. Admiral Platon had used all his authority as the special envoy of the Marshal to prevent any opposition to their seizure of territory. General Barré, however, had organized a line of withdrawal from which he could open hostilities against the enemy in a few days.

Gilbert Demangeat, a sympathizer of ours and a friend of Henri d'Astier, had placed his farm at Cape Matifou at our disposal, so we now had available rudimentary buildings and a training field. Some of the troops were already camping there.

A friend of Kiko Hérelle, Dr. Louis Alcay, lent me his car, a black Peugeot 302, and Van Hecke gave me a permit to go anywhere in Algeria, and even requested that the authorities give me aid and assistance. This Peugeot was designated as "non-registered." Like those of the autos of Achiary's DST, the number plates were simply covered with black paint, with no number. I also had a paper from the

English authorities that allowed me to resupply myself with gasoline at their service station on the harbor. So we could drive anywhere and move freely between the Rue Charras and Cape Matifou, as one of the few civilian vehicles among the jeeps and the G.M.C.'s that filled the streets.

Van Hecke and Henri d'Astier had given André Beyler, the officer of the Chantiers de la Jeunesse who had waited in vain for Giraud at Blida on the night of November 7, the mission to serve as liaison between the Chantiers and us. The English, in addition to equipment and arms, were supplying food for Cape Matifou. Every day one of our vehicles, often my Peugeot, transported necessary provisions from their supply depot. Gilbert Sabatier was in charge of the administration of the camp. Tall and sturdy, with his glasses and his 35 years, he made a serious impression in our dealings with the British.

Our dearest hope had been that Pillafort after his recovery would take command of everything. In spite of our sorrow, we had to find another leader to legalize our formation and administer the unit. We thought of General de Monsabert, who, like General Mast and Colonel Jousse, found himself in a very difficult situation, since those he had arrested and against whom he had acted were still in place. Monsabert was ready to accept, on condition that the troop numbers corresponded to his rank and that the unit was designated as French. We could assure him that we already had 500 enlistments and that within a month we expected there would be 2,000 of us. After many discussions, we decided to call ourselves the "Free Corps of Africa."

Henri d'Astier and his family were now installed at 2 Rue La Fayette, at the corner of the Boulevard Saint-Saëns. I went there often to keep Henri d'Astier informed of our activity and our progress. I knew Madame d'Astier from the days of the Hôtel Terminus, and she received me like a member of the family. Henri d'Astier's son, Jean-Bernard, a young officer in the Chantiers de la Jeunesse, had come back from Morocco to help his father. He had the same distinguished features as his father, with his mother's fair coloring. His frank and cheerful character was very pleasant. In a few days we became close friends. He worked with us in organizing the Free Corps and served as liaison with the headquarters of the Chantiers. He was a year older than I was.

Cordier, who was the intimate friend, the right arm, of Henri d'Astier, lived with them. The apartment was scantily furnished, a few kitchen tables and chairs, mattresses on box springs, an extreme simplicity. At night Jean-Bernard slept on the couch springs in the dining room, Cordier on the cushions. The atmosphere was warm, welcoming. Henri d'Astier and Madame d'Astier had three blond and charming daughters: Marie-Béatrice, who was 19; Eliane, 18 and married to Capt. Louis Jobelot, a strict regular army officer and long-time friend of his father-in-law, to whom he was completely devoted; and Arlette, 17.

Roger Rosfelder had returned from his agricultural school at Sidi-bel-Abbès. He had not said a word about it, but I understood his disappointment at not having been with us. He immediately enlisted in our corps.

Our number increased every day, but there was going to be a problem. Most of us were already enrolled in other units, and a general mobilization had just been decreed by Giraud. Would our original corps refuse to accept our new assignment? General de Monsabert, who had accepted our offer, took charge of settling this problem, as did Colonel Jamilloux, a friend whom he had taken on as aide.

At the request of Colonel Jousse, I, as adjunct to Pillafort, prepared a report on our activity of November 7 and 8 and gave it to José Aboulker.

Life went on in Algiers, during the day in the midst of the swarm of Allied troops and their vehicles, and later, after curfew, in the alerts for the Axis air raids, which were becoming more and more numerous. The bombers aimed especially at the harbor and the ships, but the list of civilian victims was getting longer. A bomb fell on the Grand Lycée, and Principal Lalande was killed with his family. The population spent the nights in cellars or in improvised shelters, but one heard few reproaches. The profound patriotism of the French of Algeria had won out over the political divisions. Many still idolized Pétain but accepted the sacrifices that the resumption of the struggle imposed on them. The Moslems did not count, except for conscription.

The morale of the American and English troops was excellent. It was taken for granted that the war could only end with our total victory. The French Commando, as they continued to call it, maintained very good relations with them.

One afternoon I was seated with a few comrades on the terrace of the Coq Hardi, which, only a few meters from our command post, served as an annex for us. A group of former members of the *Jean Bart* training program came by and seated themselves at our table. Having delayed going back to metropolitan France, they were now stuck in Algiers and had been reassigned to the Siroco Center. One of them, Herdont, looked at the American soldiers strolling along the sidewalk. "I must say, I'd rather see the Fritz than these unkempt fellows," he kept repeating. I did not take him up on it. Whether he liked it or not, Herdont was now on the right side.

Yves Bouât, the comrade who had given up joining us in March 1941 because of Mers-el-Kébir, had died on November 8 at Oran, killed on the escort ship *La Surprise*. The noncom who had murdered Jean Dreyfus had been decorated. Admiral Darlan had made Dorange a Chevalier de la Légion d'Honneur. On November 23 we learned that Roosevelt had given Clark the order to keep Darlan in power provided he gave satisfaction. It was a time of cynicism.

At 26 Rue Michelet, where I often went, my friends were morose. Relations with Murphy were becoming more and more difficult. Unpleasant words had been attributed to his entourage: we were only laborers recruited for the job. Henceforth we were officially a nuisance, men to whom one no longer knows what to say and whom one does not yet dare to usher out.

Our principal concern in those days was the squadron at Toulon. It was certain that the Germans, now that they occupied all of metropolitan France, were going to try to seize this fleet. At every moment we expected the announcement of its escape to the open sea, toward Algiers. Three battleships, 8 cruisers, 18 destroyers, 12 torpedo boats, 20 submarines, various other units, they made up a considerable force. If these vessels made their way to Algiers, France would again take her place beside the Allies. She would be able to assert herself with the great powers and be guaranteed a seat at the great international conferences.

At the urging of the Americans, who feared that this powerful squadron would fall into the hands of the enemy, Darlan sent a message to the fleet suggesting that it go, not to Algiers (which would have been too much to expect) but to Dakar, a more neutral ground that would allow it to wait for a favorable turn of events. That was just like Darlan. As usual since the armistice, he was trying to keep his fleet, his creation, outside the theater of operations, without realizing that after the war its existence would be determined by the battles it had fought and the role it had played.

The reply from Admiral Laborde was an abrupt refusal: "Neither Algiers nor Dakar!" At Vichy, Pétain and Laval declared Darlan guilty of

a felony, but we knew that the sailors of the Admiralty had a connection
by secret cable with Vichy and that by this channel Darlan exchanged
messages with Vichy in which — was it a double game or profound conviction? — he was acting as an accomplice.

On November 27, news of a disaster reached Algiers like a clap of thunder: at Toulon the fleet had scuttled itself. At dawn the German forces,
which had surrounded the roadstead, launched an attack, and almost all the
French ships sent themselves to the bottom. Only a few units fell intact
into enemy hands. After Mers-el-Kébir, Toulon. Twenty years of effort by
French taxpayers had been sacrificed by the stubbornness of a few who,
living in a vacuum, had taken as their own what was national property.
They had stupidly destroyed something that had been constructed at great
expense and entrusted to them, to serve and preserve the freedom of a
nation and not the phobias of a caste. After this lamentable suicide, France
had only Force X, the smaller squadron that had been at Alexandria at the
time of the 1940 armistice and which had refused to continue the struggle.
It had been disarmed there under English supervision, and since then it
had been rotting away, still refusing to join the battle. The Americans and
the English pretended to be sad, but they were relieved by the scuttling.
They had feared above all that the fleet might fall into the hands of the
Axis and threaten their naval supremacy in the Mediterranean. That we
should be deprived of it was the least of their concerns.

The submarine *Casablanca*, thanks to its commander, L'Herminier,
managed to leave Toulon in the middle of the German attack and to reach
Algiers. That warmed our hearts, and it showed that, even at the last
minute, it was still possible for those in charge of these ships to choose
their fate.

In Tunisia, General Barré began to fight back against the Germans, who
were still receiving numerous reinforcements in men and equipment.

At the Rue Charras, we were surmounting a lot of difficulties, but others remained. We had weapons, munitions, equipment, but scarcely any
combat uniforms; the English were slow in supplying us with them; they
had none at the moment. Even if the training followed its course at the
Demangeat farm, no one would help us reach the front line being formed
in Tunisia. Many of us were receiving recall orders from our former units,
which paid no attention to our enlistment in the Free Corps. That was
my situation. I received my recall order for the Siroco Center, and I responded by sending a duplicate of my enlistment. The reply was not long

in coming: "Your enlistment is not valid; you must join your unit immediately." Naturally I did not comply but, like many of my comrades, I was in a delicate situation. If we had been in Tunisia, no one would have come to get us.

We were beginning to learn more about the epic-making expedition of General Jacques Leclerc across Africa, about General Pierre Koenig at Bir-Hakeim, and about the exploits of the Free French forces. It was with them that we wanted to be and not in this quagmire of Algiers, where a thousand suspicious schemes were being contrived. The Americans had gone after Giraud because they wanted to have nothing to do with de Gaulle; then they accepted Darlan because a valet is easier to manipulate; but could they still believe that that was the way to play the role of liberator? Inevitably, in a normal reaction, our thoughts turned in spite of our wishes to General de Gaulle.

In his high commissariat, Darlan formed a sort of government whose ministers had the title of secretary. Under pressure from the Americans, he agreed to include in it three members of the Group of Five. Saint-Hardouin was secretary of Foreign Affairs, with his friend La Tour du Pin as assistant; Jean Rigault was secretary of the Interior. Both of them passed for having gone over to the Admiral, but the complex plotting made it impossible to have a clear idea. We asked Henri d'Astier to accept the post offered to him as adjunct secretary of the Interior, mainly responsible for police forces and counterintelligence. Thus we were not completely isolated. Now he was in a position to speak and act in dealing with French and Allied authorities. Although his power over many of his subordinates remained very theoretical, Achiary's DST now had official status; we in the Free Corps were receiving all his support.

These last few days, moreover, Henri d'Astier had seen his position strengthened. His brother François, a general in the air force, succeeded in leaving Vichy at the time of the invasion of the Free Zone and in reaching London, where he was now an aide to General de Gaulle. His brother Emmanuel had become one of the principal leaders of the Resistance in metropolitan France.

Alfred Pose, a financier and friend of the Group of Five, was secretary of Finance. Jacques Brunel had created an intelligence service at the Rue Ampère, in close liaison with Henri d'Astier and Cordier.

One morning early, as I was going down in my 302 from Hydra toward the city, I came upon a checkpoint set up by the gendarmes at the Voirol Column. They announced that they had an order to arrest me and to hand me over to the military police of the navy. I showed them my enlistment papers for the Free Corps and the permit to circulate that Van Hecke had drawn up for me. "You owe me aid and assistance," I told them.

Although they had not completely digested the coup of November 8, especially their humiliation at having been arrested by ordinary policemen, they dared go no further. When I put my car in gear, one of them shouted at me, "He's dead, huh? The Jew!"

Perhaps they had confused Dreyfus with Temime.

Luckily the mission of arresting me was not entrusted to the Mobile Guards. Their resentment toward us was manifest. When we passed by the posts where they were on guard, those who recognized us looked at us with concentrated hatred. A few days earlier, they could not deny themselves the pleasure of jumping on Germain and putting handcuffs on him. It took several hours to get him freed.

Not at all willing to find myself in Fort d'Estrée, from which it would no doubt be more difficult to extract me, I told Henri d'Astier and Van Hecke about my problem. André Beyler went to the Admiralty with a letter from General de Monsabert and obtained an order to let me alone. Cordier and Beyler settled the cases of other comrades of the Free Corps who were also considered to be deserters from their old regiments. For some, arrangements could be made; others, to avoid arrest, could not leave the Demangeat farm, where no authority dared to enter.

One morning at Mont-Hydra, as I greeted my father before leaving for the day, he showed me a large headline in the newspaper. "Listen," he said. And then he read: "Here is the lamentable tale of young fanatics whose aberration has led them to treason. Nine young men of Algiers, refusing to admit the return of France to the war on the side of the Allies and nourishing criminal feelings in favor of the Axis, recently joined the German troops in Tunisia, offering themselves for any wartime mission on the side of the enemy. The German high command, after having provided them with equipment, explosives, a radio set, and an excellent pistol for each one, had them dropped from a swastika-marked plane for a mission of spying and sabotage of railroads and Allied installations. Immediately denounced by the loyal population and arrested, after full confessions they were referred to a court martial and executed."

Nine names followed, among them Roubart, Big Roubart, who had beaten the Jews in the old days on the Rue Michelet.

"These are perhaps the same judges who would have sent you to the gallows if the landing had failed," said my father. "I wonder if the person who wrote this article had the courage to reread what he was saying a short time ago in the same newspaper."

General Mast and Colonel Barril had to take refuge in the Near East. In Morocco, General Béthouart, Colonel Magnan, and Lieutenant Gromand were arrested by General Noguès, who wanted to have them shot because they had helped in the Allied landing. General Eisenhower saved them just in time. In Algiers we ourselves could only deter the attacks against us by continual vigilance.

At the Rue Charras and Cape Matifou, little upsetting events were taking place. When I arrived at the Demangeat farm, I found two officer candidates, doubtless newly enrolled, in the office. I began to discuss the problems of the day with them. In an arrogant, offhand tone, one of them asked me, "What is your rank?"

"Adjunct to Captain Pillafort."

They pretended not to have heard me and talked to each other, ignoring my presence.

At the Rue Charras another officer candidate occupied the enlistment office. I noticed that he managed not to enroll a Jew who had arrived to volunteer, by answering him coldly, "We are taking no more enlistments; we're full."

"Perhaps you've been poisoned by propaganda, but you've gone far enough," I told him. He assumed a satisfied air and made it clear that he would take no orders from me.

Bernard Pauphilet, whose job was becoming more and more difficult, told me that, if it was going to be like that, he and Arguillère would find themselves another place to go. Those of us who had laid the foundations of the volunteer corps were outraged and disgusted, and we began to fear that our elimination was already in progress. We had no officer's stripes with which to oppose the newcomers. We were not numerous enough. If only Pillafort had been there. . . .

One morning, arriving at the Rue Charras, I found an English colonel seated at a desk, filling out weapons permits for the principal ones among us. Captain Bire was there: he was an old veteran, a faithful companion of Pillafort.

"This man absolutely needs one," he said when he saw me.

The colonel filled out a form in my name, green paper, thick, with the dry seals of the British high command.

I thought of José, Libine, of those at number 26. "I have some comrades for whom a permit is also indispensable."

The colonel showed me that his book of stubs was all used up. "I have instructions only for here," he said. I had been lucky again.

Early in the afternoon I went to number 26 to show them my permit. Perhaps they could get one. José and Bernard Karsenty were absent. I had scarcely come in when I found myself before a sort of tribunal presided over by Raphaël, seated behind a desk. Fanfan was at his side; Germain, Roger Morali, and Benhamou were there. They all had sour faces.

"You have a permit to bear arms?" demanded Raphaël.

"Yes."

"Thanks a lot!" from Fanfan.

The atmosphere was charged. They were sad, hostile. I realized what they had been enduring since November 9. It was doubtless even worse than before the landing, which had been like a beacon, a promised land with a clear purpose. Now they could rightly think that there would never be any change. Their despair, the certainty in their hearts that they would always be rejected, relegated to the ghetto, led them to suspect one who was almost their only friend. More than my condemnation, it was their own suffering that they were expressing. Plunged into a morose self-pity distilled by centuries of oppression, now they were almost reassured by my "betrayal," which restored things to order. This way, there was no exception; they were truly the accursed race, and I was not their friend. It seemed as if in an instant all that our common struggle had built up had just been swept away. I was cast back to the other side of this abject wall that I had thought was in ruins a few years ago and that Naziism had reconstructed, probably for a long time. I should have told them that, but I was tired. I didn't even think of justifying myself.

Suddenly Germain, who adored this kind of situation, pulled out two pistols and aimed them at his companions. "Nobody will touch him! Mario, you are free to go," he shouted.

Facing them theatrically, a weapon still pointed at them, he opened the door. We both went out. "You have made me very sad," he said to me on the stairway.

The next day, in town, I met Professor Aboulker. He had heard about it, and he was distressed and certain that this misunderstanding would soon be forgotten. In fact, in a few days I was seeing my friends again, and no one alluded to the incident.

I often went to the d'Astier home. The atmosphere there was pleasant, informal. Everyone called Cordier with familiarity "the abbé." The children used the "vous" form of address with their parents; the girls would say, "I promise it," instead of "I swear it." They often kept me for a meal, but most of the time we all went together to have lunch at the Paris, the restaurant of our loyal friend Louis Lalanne.

It was an agreeable and stylishly decorated place, where we found a sympathetic, relaxing atmosphere. We often met Jacques Brunel there, and Marc Jacquet, office manager for Pose at the Finance secretariat; Joxe, a former history professor now assistant to Saint-Hardouin; Capitant, an academic and official representative of those in Algiers who were leaning toward de Gaulle; General and Madame Bouscat; and many others. It was a place that was safe and out of reach of spies. Lalanne had been one of us since the beginning. His hotel, Hôtel Albert, opposite the restaurant on the other side of Lafferrière Square, had often, before the landing, sheltered certain of our friends from the English intelligence service or the Polish network whom Vichy was trying to track down. While eating, Jean-Bernard and I would speak of our problems with the Free Corps, or mingle in the general conversation. We perceived that our elders accepted the present state of affairs no more than we did. All of our discussions revolved around four words, "What can we do?"

Henri d'Astier was a little annoyed. "In any case, we're getting nowhere with this chatter."

"And do you have an idea, Mario?" Cordier asked me.

I answered that my greatest desire would be to wash my hands of everything and go to join at last a fighting unit of the Free French.

"You don't think that, as things are, it would be a kind of desertion?"

The conversation came around to General de Gaulle. The d'Astiers did not seem to be particularly attracted to him. "We have many friends who knew him well before the war," said Madame d'Astier. "He is an unbe-lievable egocentric, incorrigibly self-centered. He thinks that everything is his due, never accepts criticism or advice. He has no friends; you can't stand him. And that is why so few volunteers have joined him."

Henri d'Astier spoke of his functions as minister of police: "I'm not even able to sign the papers connected with my position. In some ways I'm only a hostage in a Vichy regime unchanged except for the fact that it is under the tutelage of the Americans. I watch, disgusted, the intrigues and the wasteful struggles for influence. These are just discredited factions intent on keeping their jobs and doing nothing to defend the interests of France against the pragmatism of our allies. Every day an unbearable sit-uation gets more and more firmly established."

Henri d'Astier was not the kind to accept all that for much longer, nor was Cordier. Side by side for two years, in the shadows, they had carried on an obstinate struggle. A few months after the armistice, when they were attached to the intelligence section of the general staff of the Oran divi-sion, they had very quickly realized that they held the same ideas and goals. Shortly afterward, because his health needed special care, Cordier was invited by the d'Astiers to live with them in their apartment on the Boulevard de Strasbourg. In April 1941 they already envisioned the possi-bility of an American landing in North Africa. Very quickly they suc-ceeded in meeting Knight and Rounds, U.S. vice consuls at Oran. These contacts, simply polite in the beginning, evolved into more frequent meet-ings in which the plan for an Allied landing took shape little by little. Together with Captain Glorieux, Lieutenant Schellenberg, and Captain Jobelot, who was to become the husband of Eliane d'Astier, they secretly organized a network in the very heart of the Vichy army, and then civilian networks with the help of a young industrialist, Roger Carcassonne. In close liaison with the British secret service and with a large network formed by Polish officers assigned to residence in Algeria and directed by Colonel Scewalski, this group was for many months the Algerian center of what was not yet called the Resistance. Many Allied agents were saved from capture thanks to the escape route to Gibraltar by way of the Habibas Islands.

Before eagerly signing on with Henri d'Astier in preparation for the landing, Cordier had already rendered important service to the cause he served by moving back and forth with cat-like skill between the leaders of Military Security and the networks with which he was in close contact.

When he was working at Military Security in Algiers at the beginning of 1941, he had managed to uncover conversations between Vichy leaders and Navy Captain Farina, head of the maritime section of the Italian armistice commission. He had learned that the Vichy government was preparing the escape from Alexandria of Force X, the French fleet quarantined there by the British for refusing to agree to continue the struggle. The commander of this fleet had secretly perfected a plan of action to break through the entrances to the harbor and reach the open sea and then Toulon. But he needed a supply of oil at sea off Crete. The Vichy government had asked Captain Farina to authorize the *Tarn*, a large tanker with full tanks, then blocked at Algiers, to go to a position in the eastern Mediterranean to wait for Force X and deliver the supplies. Naturally, after an exchange of telegrams with Rome and Berlin, the authorization had been granted.

The consequences of such an enterprise could only be catastrophic: a brutal encounter with the English and support for the Axis forces, which would be fatal to us. Without losing a moment, Cordier had succeeded in warning the Polish network, the working arm of British intelligence in Algiers. Colonel Stravikosky and Lieutenant Lubiensky had direct radio contact with London: the *Tarn* had reached the open sea but was immediately damaged by the Royal Navy and forced to return to Algiers. The supervision of Force X was increased; Vichy had to give up.

Two years of desperate struggle, then the fabulous action of November 7 and 8. And now there was bitterness and disappointment, above all a realization that the hardest part remained to be done: to give some meaning to all that had been accomplished.

On December 7, 1942, by decree, Darlan proclaimed himself head of the French State in North Africa and commander in chief of the naval, land, and air forces of the AFN. He formed an imperial council composed of Noguès, resident general in Morocco; Giraud, commander in chief of the French troops in North Africa; Yves Chatel, governor general of Algeria; Boisson, governor general at Dakar; Bergeret, air minister. Before acting he had obtained the assent of the United States, and the English had signified their agreement.

Giraud had lost all opportunity to have any influence. He pretended to concern himself only with the problems of the campaign in Tunisia, abandoning to others the political scene, in which he said he would not take part, but from which he was, in reality, excluded. He had never attempted anything whatever to help us, nor to open the concentration camps, from which no prisoners had been liberated, in spite of our pleas to the Americans, who reacted unenthusiastically, "not wishing to be embroiled in French affairs."

With Noguès, Bergeret, Boisson, Chatel, proven accomplices of collaboration, Darlan did not have to fear a palace revolution. While his authority appeared now to be on a firm foundation, everywhere a muted hostility seemed nevertheless to be rising against him. In a few days it would unfurl as open hatred. The Admiralty was his last bastion.

The French Army of North Africa, with more than 100,000 men, was deeply divided, at least in respect to the officers, for the opinion of the common soldiers was of little importance. Rigidly faithful to the Marshal or beginning to have doubts, favorable to the landing now that it was over or wishing to have things as they were before, determined to fight the Germans at the earliest possible moment or favoring a policy of waiting while the Allies bore the costs and reaped the benefits of war — all these positions were in conflict. The only points on which they agreed were their Gaullist phobia and their disgust with Darlan.

The pro-Nazi collaborators, the militant wing and strong arm of Vichy in Algeria, were at first hopeful, having reason to suppose that Darlan was leading a double game and still secretly favored the Axis designs. This period had ended. Darlan could no longer do much for his former friends; he could only turn his coat inside out once more if the fortunes of war should again become unfavorable to the Allies. It appeared clear to everyone that the Americans had found him to be a docile servant, and for the extremists of the SOL and the PPF, of whom only a few had been neutralized by Achiary, Darlan was a traitor. Some of them were thinking of assassinating him.

Several men in power, less tainted than Darlan by collaboration, were afraid of being dragged into his downfall, which seemed inevitable sooner or later. Now that these people were still holding their jobs, their chances of staying afloat appeared to them to be better but for this burdensome rotten apple.

In his position, Achiary possessed information that certain Axis agents might intend to shoot Darlan down, not to punish him for changing masters — they were practical enough not to be so attached to the past — but because they imagined that the disappearance of the admiral would produce a chaotic situation favorable to their designs.

Finally, among us, partisans who had opened our gates to the Americans, the scorn that we felt for Darlan had been replaced by an extremely powerful and deep sense of having been cheated. Our action had ended in a result contrary to our hopes and to our written agreement with the Americans. The catastrophe was due to a single man, Darlan. No one else could have played this game. We had assumed crushing responsibilities; it was our job to redress the situation. With each one of us, at all levels, this idea became so strong that it was almost our only preoccupation. At the Rue Charras, at Cape Matifou, on the terrace of the Coq Hardi, plans of action were being elaborated.

Darlan's security at the Summer Palace lay principally in the hands of the Mobile Guards. The Admiralty, where he went almost every day, was an impregnable fortress. When he traveled between the Summer Palace and the Admiralty, he had only a limited escort, only a second car and some motorcycles. He had gone several times through the Rue Michelet to get to the Rue Monge. I knew his blue eyes, almost violet in color, his cunning and hypocritical features. I often thought of the incredible opportunity that had been offered to him in June 1940. Titular head of an intact French fleet, he had held in his hands the destiny and honor of his country; he could have kept the entire Empire in the fight. Everything would have been simple then. Worn out by the mediocrity of the ministerial cabinets in which almost all of his career had taken place, his only passion was the fleet, his collection of art objects; in trying to protect them at all cost, he had condemned them to an inglorious destruction.

By the stairways of the Rue Berlioz, two steps away from our command post, we had an easy back route for breaking out in force into the Rue Monge at the moment when Darlan's car passed. Blocking the road and killing Darlan would be easy. We just had to be willing to do it. Our idea was not to hide what we were doing but to act in broad daylight and in large numbers, thus openly claiming responsibility for our act. Then, if we could, we would take refuge at the farm on Cape Matifou under the protection of the British, if they were willing, then go without delay to fight in Tunisia. We would ask to be judged by a French court at the end of the war.

This plan was approved by more than a sufficient number of us, but the risk of also killing innocent people made us hesitate. There were always lots of people present at his customary time of passing, which coincided with the closing time of the girls' *lycée*. Furthermore many American and English soldiers would be walking about in the Rue Michelet. We studied all the ways to avoid a useless spilling of blood; we even considered sparing the motorcycle riders, but of course we could not be certain. To tell the truth, we had not absolutely made up our minds. At Cape Matifou, others organized action groups with similar plans.

For two or three days, Pierre-Marie Cordier had been absent. On the morning of December 10, I found him at the apartment on the Rue La Fayette. I was preparing to leave with Jean-Bernard to join Roger and Kiko for a trip out to Cape Matifou when Cordier said he wanted to speak to me. We sat down on the sofa.

"Mario, we have often discussed the present situation without finding a way out. Everyone here is divided; each one refuses to accept the authority of the others. De Gaulle is in London — many people here have to accept Darlan's protection — the navy, whose morale is low, the army cliques — all these factions paralyze each other. We must put the pieces back together and rebuild unity, if we are to resume the struggle against the Axis and prepare for the future with any success. The liberation of France must not end in a disastrous civil war, the worst of all outcomes. We need a unifying element, something or someone acceptable to everyone. So I ask you, what or who might this element or this person be? I am sure you already have his name on your lips."

I was perplexed; the name that came to mind was that of de Gaulle, although he was obviously far from being a unifying element acceptable to everyone.

"De Gaulle," I finally said.

Cordier appeared disappointed. "You know that de Gaulle, in the present state of affairs, cannot unite us. On the contrary. Today he is isolated, divisive. He must absolutely accept the authority of this person. Now do you see who I mean?"

"I still don't see any better."

He was surprised, somewhat amused, as if I were deliberately denying the obvious. "Come now, Mario! Why, the Count of Paris!"

I was stunned. "But no one even knows where he is!"

"He is in the next room," answered Cordier.

Now I understood why Cordier had not been here. He explained that this idea had taken shape in the course of Henri d'Astier's conversations with Alfred Pose, Jean Van Hecke, Marc Jacquet, and Pierre Alexandre, representing the Jewish community of metropolitan France. It seemed to them that the person of the Count of Paris had a strong possibility of reconciling the bitter factions. In a car belonging to the Chantiers, driven by Van Hecke's chauffeur, Ponchon, Cordier had gone to Morocco with orders signed by General de Monsabert. The prince, who was waiting at Oujda, agreed to come to Algiers with him, accompanied by his aide de camp, the director of the BNCI of Oujda. They had arrived early that morning.

Cordier asked me if I was ready to help in this enterprise.

"And what will you do about Darlan?" I asked.

"We hope Darlan will understand that he is the one who is preventing reconciliation and that the time has come for him to get out of the way. People highly placed in his entourage are going to try to persuade him."

A fraternal friendship linked me to Cordier, and I said he could count on me. He went into the next room, while Jean-Bernard and I exchanged a few words with Madame d'Astier and her daughters, who had joined us in the dining room. In spite of all their adventures, which had made them as calm as old soldiers, they were somewhat excited by the presence of the Count of Paris.

"The trip was tiring — all that way. When the car went through Bourkika, at dawn, His Lordship was afraid he was recognized," said Madame d'Astier.

I reassured them, laughing. No one at Bourkika, a little village of the Mitidja, had the slightest idea that the Count of Paris existed.

I went to meet Denise as she came out of the girls' *lycée*. She was 16, blond and pretty, and graceful as well. She had big blue eyes, a charming nose, and a little pointed chin. We walked for a moment along the paths of Guynemer Square, and I told her about the arrival of the Count of Paris. She did not seem surprised. After all, this solution was no more preposterous than many others to which the history of France had accustomed us.

In the evening I made my father play Cordier's guessing game. He could not come up with the name of the wonderful unifier and was somewhat taken aback when I revealed our new plans to him.

"In Algiers, it's true, anything is possible at this moment," he said, "but the responsibilities that you are assuming must not lead you to imprudent acts. Even if you succeed, what will metropolitan France think about your way of solving the problem?"

He recognized, however, that if de Gaulle, Giraud, and the major factions that were not too deeply involved in the collaboration lined up under the banner of the Count of Paris, that might provide a solution that would make reconciliation necessary, even if only temporary.

"But first of all Darlan must withdraw," he added. "And that kind of man never understands that the time has come. He's going to hang on, you can be sure."

Henri d'Astier and Cordier had no funds to meet the various expenses of putting these plans into action. I asked my father for money, and the next day he gave me 100,000 francs. "And even if what happens proves that you are wrong, I will think that you have done the right thing."

I gave the money to Cordier, who was overjoyed. He put the bills in a table drawer and then showed them to friends who came by: "Here is our war chest!"

The Count of Paris lodged first in the Chemin Beaurepaire with the Count de Tocqueville, then at the Rue La Fayette in the bedroom of the d'Astiers, who had retreated to their daughters' room. With complete simplicity he took part in the life of the household, even sometimes helping Madame d'Astier and her daughters wash the dishes. He often went to the Algéria, a big white building farther up the Boulevard Saint-Saëns where Marc Jacquet and René Davhernas, assistant for economic affairs in the office of Alfred Pose, had their apartments. The prince's aide de camp lived with Davhernas. Cordier asked me if I wanted to be presented to the prince, but I answered that there was no need. We passed in the hall or on the sidewalk when he went for a walk on the Rue Michelet or the Boulevard Saint-Saëns, wearing a camel's hair coat. Glasses with very black lenses made him unrecognizable.

Although I was not much involved in the dealings now in progress, I nevertheless understood that many consultations were taking place. At the Rue La Fayette there was a continual coming and going of politicians and generals in civilian clothes. Many conversations were held at the Algéria. Marc Jacquet and Pierre Alexandre were particularly active.

The religious devotion of the d'Astier family, always discreet but also profound, had increased. Except for Jean-Bernard, who preferred my company, they went to mass every day, and usually Madame d'Astier returned for vespers. Their church was Saint-Augustin. For them almost everything took place on a spiritual level, impartially, at a distance. Whatever happened was in God's hands.

The Count of Paris was also very pious. Cordier had brought back from the Saint-Augustin church a little portable altar, where His Lordship could attend his daily mass without danger of being recognized. He was the only one to take precautions, since the law forbade him to live on French territory. If Darlan had chanced to learn of these secret meetings, he could have had the prince expelled or even arrested him. But we had to believe that the Admiral was really isolated if he had not heard of all these comings and goings, meetings, conferences held in 20 different places, in which many of his entourage were participating. Everything was still highly secret, it was true, as if it had been a synod whose prelates were spread around the city.

I saw Henri d'Astier very little these days and only briefly, but Cordier kept me informed. Everything was going well; everyone in Algiers was in agreement, or at least ready to accept the outcome if things went well. The principal local politicians now gave their approval, among them Amédée Froger, president of the general council, liberal, very influential, one of the notables who, as early as November 26, with a group of deputies and general councilors, had called upon Darlan in writing to withdraw. The Catholic clergy and the Grand Master of the Masonic Lodge of Algiers were in favor, and Alexandre reported the agreement of the Jews. General Juin, as well as a large number of the army leaders, were willing to see a Council of the Empire formed, presided over by the Count of Paris, in which everyone, maintaining his dignity, could move in any direction necessary. The accession of the prince to the presidency of this Council of the Empire would be accomplished in legal form. On December 18, the three presidents of the general councils of Algeria, Amédée Froger, Saurin, and Dyron, would go to the Summer Palace and read their summons to Darlan. Reiterating the terms of their letter of November 26, which had remained unanswered, they would summon him, this time solemnly, to withdraw.

"You are fulfilling none of the conditions which confer on you the powers of a legal and independent government. It is impossible for you to obtain from the Allied powers the guarantees necessary to the future of our country. When the legitimate government cannot exercise its authority, the law of February 15, 1872, called the law of Tréveneuc, stipulates that it is the responsibility of the general councils of the departments that have remained free to choose the head of government. We demand therefore that you give your resignation into our hands so that we may apply the law with full respect for the constitution."

Everyone supposed that Darlan would have to give in. He might even think that these overtures provided an ideal exit for him. The Americans would be faced with a fait accompli. After the resignation of Darlan, the general councils would take note of the power vacuum and, according to the constitution, would establish a provisional government in anticipation of regular elections. The first act of this government would be to annul the Darlan-Clark accords.

At the Rue La Fayette, on a morning when the apartment had recovered its calm now that the regular meetings and conferences were taking place at the Algéria or in the drawing rooms of the Hôtel Aletti, Cordier and I talked together.

"Mario, you said you were sure that Darlan's immediate entourage would unite around him; well, I can tell you that that's not the case. The Count of Paris had a conversation yesterday with General Bergeret, and at the end of it Bergeret declared to the prince that he was personally placing himself under his orders. The Count of Paris is satisfied with the progress of our plans, and he has expressed the wish that his election to the presidency of this national government should take place without delay, so that on December 24 the midnight mass at the cathedral of Algiers can be followed by a solemn *Te Deum* to celebrate the reconciliation of all Frenchmen."

Cordier took a typewritten paper out of his pocket. "This is the declaration that the prince is intending to make, once he takes power. I'm the one who drew it up. I'll read it to you."

"In response to the appeal of the three French departments which have remained free, and according to the wish of the army, I now take power. A true Frenchman, I do not come as a partisan. I hold to no flag other than that of our native land, which is prostrate and wounded. I am here to save it, to unite all those who aspire likewise to liberate it from the invader. I am the unifier of French energy. The hour has come to unite by law what is united in fact.

"You will judge, then, and the people of France with you, what form of government to give to our country, so that it may remain strong but without ceasing to be humane, so that it may reconcile its taste for liberty with the discipline that life demands."

Cordier looked at me to see what I thought. I told him that it was lacking in character, that it was "cat food."

"That's what we need," he said. Then, a bit condescending, sure of himself, he added, "You have to understand: we are establishing a symbol, so I wrote a symbolic speech."

I pointed out that until now Henri d'Astier and he himself had given me the impression that they were not particularly attached to the person of the prince.

"It seems that you have somewhat confused the notions of 'person' and 'concept,'" he remarked in an analytic tone, leaning back in his armchair. "If you wish, let's first discuss the concept. Henri and I are very attached to it, but we would never have planned to put it into practice even in this form, which has nothing to do with a restoration, if events had not forced us to. True, we sincerely believe that a constitutional dynasty can protect a nation from deplorable accidents like the dictatorship of Hitler, for example. We are convinced that management by a normal being surrounded if possible by competent people, even if they are difficult, is more likely to secure a nation's well-being than a rise to power, by trickery or force, of paranoids or adventurers, which is possible in the vacuum of unstructured regimes.

"All right, now let's consider the 'person.' Henri and I aren't complaining. He is an Orléans, of a royal family, with a gentle, diffident character. If the prince did not have a profound notion of his duty toward his country and his House, if he were not aware that he is the only means to rescue France from a situation that seems insurmountable, he would probably have refused to come to Algiers, preferring the tranquility of his estate in Larache, in Spanish Morocco, to an adventure of this kind. We are glad that he is willing to expose his 'person,' but, believe me, Henri and I are not followers of any cult. Our faith is on a higher plane. It was Marc Jacquet who first had the idea of turning to the Count of Paris, and Henri was reticent at first. Do you know what he said to Madame d'Astier after his first conversation with the prince? 'He's not as bad as I thought, after all.' "

Secret messages had been exchanged with de Gaulle, who seemed ready to take this proposal into consideration. Anyway, he would accept no one other than the Count of Paris to be in authority over him. The latter, for his part, gave the impression of not trying in any way to provoke a restoration of the monarchy. He came to help in uniting us, to offer to arbitrate.

General François d'Astier was supposed to arrive at any minute from London to settle details for the plan of government to be drawn up by the general councils. Under the authority of the Count of Paris, the governing power would go to General de Gaulle, and the military command to General Giraud. Henri d'Astier's brother would have been here already if Darlan and those faithful to him had not persuaded the Americans to postpone his trip.

The admiral rejected the proposal to receive the delegation from the general councils, which Saint-Hardouin had transmitted to him. To use force to obtain this interview would be to get involved in an adventure with grave consequences, since on December 17 Eisenhower had declared that he would oppose militarily any coup against Darlan. In any case, everyone was opposed to the use of force, anxious above all that this Council of the Empire be constituted legally. Other means had to be found.

Henri d'Astier, as minister of police and counterintelligence, flooded Darlan with reports of many assassination plans, concluding that these threats would certainly materialize if he did not resign in the next few days. We had to admit that so far the admiral had remained as hard as stone.

The walls of Algiers were covered with inscriptions hostile to Darlan. When we read in big letters painted with tar, "The admiral to the fleet," we knew that the fellows who were taken prisoner at the Admiralty had passed by. ["L'amiral à la flotte" provides a typical French pun, as it can also mean "Throw the admiral into the sea."] "Death to the traitor Darlan" was probably the work of impenitent Vichyites. "Darlan, we're going to get you" could be from anyone.

Jean-Bernard asked me to get him a weapon. I still had my Hersthal 7.65 stuck in my belt, and the 6.35 that Pillafort gave me was a kind of sacred relic for me. There remained the Rubis 7.65 that I had taken from the naval officer, but since it wasn't working very well I took it to an armorer near the Opéra, at the entrance to the Rue Bab-Azoun. I showed him my permit to bear arms, and he wrote my name on his register, with the nature of my permit and the number of the weapon, and told me to come back in two days.

On December 19, General François d'Astier de la Vigerie arrived in Algiers. It was a quiet visit, almost secret. Thanks to General Eisenhower, de Gaulle had at last been able to establish this liaison. In trouble with the American news correspondents in Algiers, and criticized by the New York press, which reproached him strongly for his agreements with Darlan, Eisenhower seemed at last to perceive that things were not as simple as he had thought at first.

Toward the end of the evening, after returning from the Demangeat farm, I stopped in at the Rue La Fayette. Henri d'Astier and Madame d'Astier, Cordier, and Alfred Pose were in the dining room. Pose was dressed in a long navy blue cape that came down beyond his ankles and was wearing the cap of an air force general. As he was short, pudgy, with a large nose, a mischievous glance, and a playful manner in spite of his more than 50 years, his appearance was rather comical. He was playing the clown, gesticulating, taking poses, to amuse his friends. The cape and cap belonged to François d'Astier.

Cordier said that as soon as he arrived the general had told his brother that the main object of his trip was a private meeting with the Count of Paris. "General de Gaulle has given me the mandate to deal directly with the prince," he declared.

As the prince had been in bed for two days with an attack of malaria, the general had come to the Rue La Fayette. Both were at this moment in the d'Astiers' bedroom.

Pose took off the cape and sat down. Suddenly subdued, he remarked, "Well, they have been talking for two hours. . . . They must really have something to say."

Madame d'Astier, Henri d'Astier, and Cordier, sitting around the table, kept silent, and I felt that they were somewhat concerned about the outcome of the conversation. I left so as not to risk embarrassing them.

The next morning Cordier told me what he knew about the course of the conversation. Before leaving the apartment, General d'Astier had expressed his satisfaction with his talk with the prince, and he had mentioned General de Gaulle's agreement concerning the Algiers plan. The Count of Paris had also showed joy and optimism. Today General d'Astier had seen Jacques Lemaigre-Dubreuil and then General Giraud. With Eisenhower, he had encountered more understanding and friendliness than he had expected: the American supreme commander now seemed to realize more clearly the degree to which the Darlan expedient would be morally prejudicial to a solution of the political problems that would accompany the battles of liberation. General d'Astier seemed to be strongly impressed by the heavy atmosphere that hovered over Algiers and by the persecution of all who had arranged for the Allied intervention. He observed, in the course of a conversation with Capitant, the stifled restlessness that it was creating. Murphy, adding his view, insisted that he should see Darlan.

On December 21, Cordier, whom I saw again at the Rue La Fayette, appeared very anxious. The interview with Darlan had gone very badly. The general, who thought he was going to talk with Darlan alone, found himself in the presence of several judges who did not hide their hostility. Bergeret assumed the role of principal spokesman for Darlan. Giraud insisted on practical details. The admiral, nervous, curt, asserted that he was the one who held power, that he would not let go, that the only concession he would make would be to grant amnesty to those who had helped the Allies. He accused General d'Astier of having come to Algiers to create disorder.

"Well, what are we going to do? What can the Count of Paris do under the circumstances?" I wondered.

Cordier shrugged in a gesture of impotence. He looked very tense, and I had the impression that he was not telling me everything. In the evening I returned to wait for Henri d'Astier to come back from his brother's room at the Hôtel Aletti. Cordier was not there, nor was Jean-Bernard. Madame d'Astier, normally relaxed and cheerful, seemed preoccupied. She informed me that the prince's health had improved and that he had gone to rest in a villa at Sidi-Ferruch, a bathing beach a few kilometers from Algiers.

Henri d'Astier came home, with his "difficult day" appearance; he was stooped, his head drooping. This time it was even more obvious than usual; he seemed tired and strained. We sat at the table; Madame d'Astier was still in the kitchen. We were alone; it was twilight, and the air raid sirens were beginning to wail. The electricity had been cut off.

"My brother François brought from London formal orders to eliminate Darlan," Henri d'Astier said, in a low voice.

I was not surprised. What other decision could they make in London? Since my last conversation with Cordier, I had thought that it would have to come to that.

"My brother has just been kicked out," continued d'Astier. "The Americans told him so just now. Everything has gone badly; it should have been expected. I am not a Gaullist, but where are we now? I know what the situation is here, but we had not given enough thought to what my brother told me. The heart of everything for us must be metropolitan France. Over there the Resistance is acting and they are dying every day under torture, or are being shot. In them we must recognize our hopes for honor and renewal. Right now those people are desperate when they see what we in Algiers have been agreeing to for weeks. From everywhere in France, London is getting messages that express fury from some, discouragement from others. The non-communist Resistance has received a shock that may prove to be fatal and will leave the field open to extremists if the present state of affairs continues. We're all that remains. Roosevelt received de Gaulle's envoys, André Philip and Tixier, on November 23. He wasn't even polite to them. He shouted, 'Of course I deal with Darlan; he has given me Algiers. Tomorrow I will deal with Laval, if he gives me Paris.' That's the democrat who says he's the liberator of the people. What we have to understand in the end is that Roosevelt and Murphy are Americans and that we are Frenchmen. We have confused alliance and friendship; we're always waiting for others to do our job."

As Madame d'Astier had come into the room to set the table, I got up; Henri d'Astier and I shook hands in the semi-darkness.

On December 22, early in the morning, I stopped at the Rue La Fayette to get Jean-Bernard. We were supposed to pick up Roger and Kiko at the Rue Charras or at the Coq Hardi on our way to Cape Matifou. Cordier was not there, but Jean-Bernard told me that he had asked me to wait. He arrived at about ten, even more tense than the evening before, his gestures more abrupt. His attitude was that of someone who has turned a page, who no longer wants to ask himself any questions. As soon as he began to speak, I realized the effort that he was making to hide his anxiety and to give an impression of calm.

"Have you noticed how time has gone by while we've been pursuing chimerical hopes? We took on responsibilities that went way beyond what we thought. If they crush us in the end, so be it, but we'll do what we have to. We've waited too long; we aren't seeing things clearly any more, all shut up with our little problems. We've lost sight of the most important part, the larger struggle we're involved in. How long could we go on without making up our minds? Well, now everything is clear."

I asked him if the fact that the order came from London meant that it emanated from Churchill.

"François d'Astier brought us de Gaulle's message. We don't know if others know about it."

"Do you think the order was to have been given only in case the negotiations failed?"

Cordier was on his feet, stiff, inflexible. "The failure was certain. The talks were only the excuse to send General d'Astier. Henri and I were wrong to hope."

"The word 'elimination' is subject to various interpretations, isn't it?"

He seemed surprised at the term. "That's Henri's euphemism. Actually, it's an order for execution."

I told him that I was with him, and that I would go to the Demangeat farm to iron out the details of the operation.

"No, that's not what has to be done."

At this moment Marc Jacquet arrived, and he immediately raised the subject. A group of officers, "flaunting their decorations," would be willing to act as a court-martial; they would occupy the offices of the Summer Palace, where Darlan was staying, arrest him, judge him, and shoot him on the spot.

"That's no good," exclaimed Cordier. "We must see to it that neither the Resistance, nor de Gaulle, nor the Count of Paris is accused. It must be seen as the act of an isolated individual. We need someone who is very sure of himself."

A little uneasy, Jacquet turned toward me. "You, Mario?"

Cordier interrupted him. "That's impossible. Mario is too well known to the Mobile Guards, to counterintelligence, to everybody. The one who executes Darlan must be someone unknown."

When Jacquet left, Cordier explained the plan that he must have been turning over and over in his mind since yesterday.

"Darlan comes every morning and every afternoon to the upper villa of the Summer Palace, near Sainte-Marie church. His office and his general staff are there. You enter by an iron gate next to the church; about 20 Mobile Guards are posted there. To pass through this gate, you have to show your identity papers and explain your reason for coming. The person doing the job will be accompanied to the entrance of the villa, where there is another guard, and will then be taken to the office of the duty orderly. Here again he'll have to present his papers, which will be false, as well as a document indicating an appointment with La Tour du Pin, who will not be there. The person will say that he wants to wait. The orderly will note his identity and the time, and the person will just go up to the second floor and wait in the open courtyard for the arrival of Darlan, who will have to pass by to go into his office. Darlan will be shot as soon as he arrives and, in the panic that is bound to follow, the person who has done the deed will open the door of Darlan's office only one meter away. This door is never locked, but it will be almost shut, so that no one can see that the office window has been opened. The person will climb out of the window, and after a short jump he only has to get over the little wall at the Chemin de Gascogne to be out of range. Before the operation, he will have been given a completely authentic passport with the same name as the identity card, and the visas necessary to go to Spanish Morocco, as well as a large sum of French and foreign money. And he will also have been given all of the instructions necessary for staying in touch with us. If the guards intervene too quickly, or if any other mishap might prevent him from getting away, the person will let himself be arrested without resistance. As soon as he is in the hands of the guards, Saint-Hardouin will declare that he must be an agent of the Axis and will give orders that he be taken immediately to the DST, where inspectors whom I have just talked with will see to the rest. At this moment they're holding several Italian spies, one of whom will try to escape; he will be shot and then recognized as Darlan's assassin. Our man will quickly leave the DST without being identified."

He looked at me in a questioning manner. Obviously it was all very clever, but the gears of the machine were so delicate that a grain of sand could wreck everything. My skepticism bothered him very much.

"And the person in question? You still have to find him."

"I was going to discuss that with you. All the information that I have indicates that many groups at Cape Matifou, at the Rue Charras, and at the Coq Hardi are ready to do anything whatever to kill Darlan."

"That's true."

"Among them are two fellows who spend their days at the Coq Hardi declaring to anyone who will listen that they will sacrifice their lives for the chance to kill Darlan. I mean Kalfort and Leplan. Do you know them?"

"Yes, everybody knows them. What you're saying is true — they never leave the Coq Hardi. In my opinion, they are fine, sincere fellows who don't have what it takes for what you are proposing."

"I prefer to find out for myself," said Cordier. "Here's what we're going to do. Early in the afternoon, you'll go to the Coq Hardi and sit at their table; you'll propose the affair to them in outline without naming any names. I will be at a nearby table, where I can listen and study their reactions."

I arrived at the Coq Hardi at about 2:30. Kalfort and Leplan were at their customary table, and as I drew near they invited me to join them. Cordier took a table nearby.

Kalfort was an Alsatian, Leplan a native of Algiers; they were somewhere between 25 and 30. Hardly had I sat down than one of them began, "And during all this time Darlan is still alive." I confided that it just so happened that I had an idea to propose to them if they were really serious. They exclaimed that they had been saying it long enough; they were ready to risk their lives if they had a real chance of succeeding. Then, in a loud voice, as if I were on a stage, so that Cordier could hear, I explained as much of the plan as necessary. They turned pale. I admit that I insisted on the small chance there was of their both coming out alive. They refused in chorus.

Cordier had already set out for the Rue La Fayette, where I soon joined him. I could see at once that he was upset.

"Well, did you see?"

"From now on, this is none of your business," he answered. Obviously he did not appreciate my sabotaging his plan. I did it instinctively, for I still preferred a commando raid in which we would take full responsibility.

"Well, anyway, they wouldn't have done it."

"This is none of your business any more," he answered in an aggrieved tone.

With Jean-Bernard I went back to Cape Matifou, and found less activity in the camp. In the last few days many enlistees in the Free Corps had been sent to Bordj-bou-Arréridj, an isolated spot in the Constantine region, on the way to Tunisia but several hundred kilometers from the front. On the pretext of moving them toward the front, they had been neutralized. We already had some dead and wounded, as the train carrying the first contingent was sabotaged. On the hill up to Miliana, the cars assigned to the volunteers of the Free Corps had mysteriously become detached from the rest of the train and coasted back down, smashing into a freight train.

On the morning of December 23 I arrived as usual at the Rue La Fayette at about nine, to find Jean-Bernard waiting for me. Cordier was there, too.

"So, have you found your 'person'?" I asked with a laugh.

"This is none of your business now. Anyway, I have the one I need."

Jean-Bernard was on the balcony; the glass door was open, as the weather was beautiful and mild. "Do you know who it is?"

"No."

"It is Bonnier de la Chapelle."

I had never seen Bonnier de la Chapelle, but we had almost met several times. During the November 8 operation he was part of the group that occupied the Agha station; then he had enrolled in the Free Corps, and he was almost always at Cape Matifou, in an action group. His father was a journalist. Roger knew him well; they were together in the Chantiers, in which Bonnier was a noncom. One day, when we were leaving the Demangeat farm in our car, Roger had said to me, "Why, there's Bonnier de la Chappelle"; but we were in a hurry and drove off. His fiancée, coincidentally, lived directly above the d'Astier family, and Bonnier often came to see her. On several occasions he had visited Henri d'Astier and Cordier. One morning, talking with Madame d'Astier, I had heard a deep voice with a distinctive note in the next room.

"That's Bonnier de la Chapelle," she had said. "You could recognize his voice among thousands." He had been with Cordier, who walked through the hallway and accompanied him to the door.

Bonnier had come to see Cordier the evening before, shortly after my departure. He announced that he had absolutely made up his mind to shoot Darlan by any means possible, and he asked Cordier to help him out. Cordier replied that he would think about it, and had then left. Bonnier, alone with Jean-Bernard, insisted that he would do it no matter what.

"My decision is irrevocable, I am determined. Furthermore, a few days ago at Cape Matifou three other comrades and I drew lots to choose which one of us would assassinate Darlan. We swore that the job would go to whoever got the longest straw. I drew the longest straw. For me there's no more discussion. I will do what I agreed to do. That's why I'm asking Cordier to help me. He is well placed to help me get it right."

Cordier came to me, apparently having forgotten last evening's argument. "Do you want to accompany me? I have an errand to do."

We left together on foot, and as we walked he said he had to meet somebody in front of Gsell Hall, which was below the university, near the girls' *lycée*. Someone was waiting, in fact, in the crowd there. From a distance, I recognized Baldacci, an inspector of the DST. Cordier went over and Baldacci slipped him an identity card, which Cordier glanced at and then put into his pocket; they moved away from each other. When we got back to the Rue La Fayette, I asked, "You're going on with your project in spite of Kalfort and Leplan?"

"What else can we do? Do you think we're in any position to add more problems? When we undertook this struggle in June of 1940, you and I, we knew it would take us a long way. Whether we like it or not, we've been caught in the mechanism. We can continue or give up, meaning betray everything and take ourselves out of the chain of action, just when we might be most useful, in order to spare our own little lives, our own little souls. Do you want to give up? All right, since we're staying with it, let's do what we must; let's respect our promise."

"And what about Bonnier?"

"Bonnier's going to act anyway. Can I refuse him the means? Do we have to be paralyzed after all we've done because this operation was not foreseen in the *Officer's Manual*?"

Is it wrong or right? That was a question that I had not often asked during those two and a half years. I had acted according to instinct and circumstances. Today, it was more difficult. For the first time I would be part of a dangerous action only as a spectator. For me, the liberty of the individual was primary. It was my struggle for liberty that had gotten me entangled in this net. Cordier, who was looking not for his own liberty but for a way to offer himself, was likewise caught in a trap. Bonnier de la Chapelle and his comrades had liberated themselves by drawing lots: maybe that was the best way to solve the problem. My fatalistic side, detached, almost indifferent, especially since Pillafort's death, was gradually getting the upper hand. That's how things were, after all. One could not become so totally engaged in a conflict that was tearing the world apart without someday becoming the prisoner of the cause that one had chosen. For years men had been dying because of this war, and here I was philosophizing.

I left Cordier at the lower end of the Boulevard Saint-Saëns and went to the armorer's to get the pistol that I had entrusted to him. I was still vaguely hoping that this plan would fall by the wayside and that we would be able to set up the commando operation in the Rue Monge.

As always whenever I was alone after November 14, the music of Beethoven kept me company. Like an obsession, the first measures of the *Fourth Symphony* came relentlessly to my mind.

The pistol was ready, and coming back to my car in the Rue La Fayette I walked along the Rue d'Isly. The happy pre-landing days came to mind, the period when the sleepy city was waiting. I retraced the route that had been customary when Pillafort, Daridan, Poulet, and I walked back and forth from the Tantonville to the Lafferrière. That time would never return. . . . It had been a time of hope.

I found Jean-Bernard and gave him the pistol. He was delighted. We went on to the Etoile on the Rue d'Isly, a brasserie that belonged to our friend Lalanne, the owner of the Paris. We were supposed to meet Henri d'Astier there and go with him to the Paris for lunch.

Upstairs at the Etoile, on a sort of vast interior balcony, were various meeting rooms that were used in normal times by different associations. Jacques Brunel had made it into an annex of his offices on the Rue Ampère. In one of these little rooms, partitioned off by translucent panels, Henri d'Astier and Jacques Brunel were engaged in a conversation. Jean-Bernard and I sat down beside them.

"Even if I'm yielding to his arguments, because it's impossible not to, I do not want de Gaulle here for the moment," Henri d'Astier was saying. "De Gaulle in Algiers will think only of himself; he'll listen to no one. I hope he'll respect the agreement more easily if the problem has already been solved ahead of time. Then he wouldn't have to come until later, to integrate himself into what we will have done, when he'll no longer be able to impose himself as omnipotent."

"Solved without him, and in a large part for him. . . . What more could he want?" answered Jacques Brunel.

"Unfortunately, it's now impossible for us not to act. You'll admit that there is something curious about the fact that we are controlled by the very person we mistrust."

Henri d'Astier was not free for lunch, so Jean-Bernard and I went without him to the Paris. As we ate, Jean-Bernard informed me that his Uncle François had brought $40,000 to his father from London. Henri d'Astier had told the general that he would give the money to Capitant. "He's the one who represents Gaullism here," he said. D'Astier was still advocating a solution by arbitration and feared an assumption of power by de Gaulle, who, in a very bad position after the landing, would now become, because of the disaster of Darlan and the incompetency of Giraud, the best recourse if plans concerning the prince did not go anywhere.

"As to the Count of Paris," I said, "does Cordier expect to present him with a fait accompli regarding the planned action? Is he informed? Does he agree?"

"Listen, my dear Mario, this is too important. . . . I think it's better that you should know, but I prefer that my mother tell you herself. Let's go to the Rue La Fayette. She'll certainly tell you what happened."

A few moments later we were at the d'Astiers'. Madame d'Astier opened the door, and going right to the point Jean-Bernard said, "Mama, I think Mario should know. Today everything is absolutely secret, but maybe someday we will be glad that he can bear witness. What do you think?"

"I think you're right. It's best that Mario be informed."

She turned to me: "We hope that, God willing, none of this will ever be known. But it is not impossible that, later on, revealing the truth may be necessary. Let's go into the bedroom. It will be easier to explain what happened if we are on the spot."

I knew this room well. Before the prince's visit, Jean-Bernard, his sisters, and I often took refuge here when too many visitors were present. The bedroom was not large and it was very simply furnished. Opposite the door was a large, plain bed, four wooden legs supporting a bedspring. In front of the bed, two chairs. On the right, the window. Between the door and the window there was a little piece of wooden furniture painted gray, three shelves that held a few books. On the other side of the door, a closet. The sunlight was filtered by a screen over the window, which looked out on the neighboring building.

Madame d'Astier then spoke. "On the day before yesterday, Monday the 21st, at about ten in the morning, the aide de camp of the Count, who had been conversing with him in this very place, informed my husband, the abbé, and me, waiting in the dining room, that His Lordship had an important communication to make and that he requested all three of us to come to him. We came into the room where we are now, and the aide de camp left the apartment. The prince, still sick with malaria, was in bed."

"In my fathers's pajamas," Jean-Bernard added.

"Because the Count had seemed to us up to now to be a little capricious and without any firm initiative, his determined and decisive manner struck us immediately," continued Madame d'Astier. "He seemed transformed. We were standing around him, my husband to the right of the bed, Cordier on the other side, and I leaning on this bookshelf, as I am doing now. The prince declared without preamble, 'I am now certain that Darlan is a traitor. Maintaining him in power prevents any solution. I order you to eliminate him without delay. Everything must be done by the 24th.' My husband then asked him what he meant by 'eliminate,' and the Count answered, 'To cause him to disappear.' Again Henri asked, 'By any means possible? Is that what you mean?' Then the prince declared, 'Yes, that is it, to make him disappear by any means possible.'"

We went back to the dining room, where Madame d'Astier resumed her account. "Totally surprised, the abbé and I were silent; Henri responded politely, acknowledging the prince's decision. But when we got back to the dining room, we didn't know what to say. Finally my husband wondered, 'How could he have changed to this degree? What happened?' But then, after a moment, he added, 'I think I'm beginning to understand. I'm to see François this afternoon; he'll give us the key to the mystery.'"

Jean-Bernard intervened. "On the day before yesterday in the early evening, in his room at the Hôtel Aletti, my uncle revealed to my father that General de Gaulle had ordered him to transmit to the Count a formal message about the need to eliminate Darlan quickly. My uncle repeated to my father what he had already reported to the Count, that is, the reasons that led de Gaulle to make this decision: no hope of carrying through the plan in progress and no hope of freedom from American control, as long as Darlan was alive. He emphasized the motive that de Gaulle considers to be most important: if Darlan is not quickly eliminated and replaced by men who have their confidence, members of the Resistance in France will fall under Soviet influence and control, which will lead to catastrophe when the territory is liberated. De Gaulle is convinced that, if necessary steps are not taken without delay, all the effort, the sacrifice, and the suffering will finally end only in the replacement of Hitler's dictatorship by that of Stalin."

"Last night, Mario, just after you left, my husband said to me confidentially, 'We no longer have a choice.' And a little later, when Cordier returned, he recounted to him his conversation with François. Then he stood up and said wearily, 'Well, Abbé, it's your play.'"

All three of us remained for a moment without saying anything. Then Madame d'Astier broke the silence. "Anyway, what can the abbé do? He would have to have tanks. . . ."

I realized that she did not know about Cordier's plan or what was being prepared with Bonnier de la Chapelle. Jean-Bernard and I said nothing. It was not for us to reveal the plans of those who placed their trust in us.

"For a prince, this determination is not so bad, after all," I said, to lighten the atmosphere. "The Count of Paris could have answered General d'Astier that he was not the secular arm of de Gaulle. On the contrary, he did not back away. He wants to cut the Gordian knot himself."

"Louis-Philippe in the role of Alexander. Don't you think there's something wrong there?" exclaimed Jean-Bernard. "I have the impression that the Count of Paris has nothing like the character of his ancestor Louis-Philippe. To me, it looks more like a tale of Charles VII and Jean Sans Peur. Jeanne d'Arc would be, let's say, Pose . . . and the councilor who gets the Dauphin to assassinate Jean Sans Peur, we know who that is now: de Gaulle!"

We had succeeded in making Madame d'Astier smile.

On the day before Christmas the weather was mild and sunny. In Algiers people were preparing for the midnight celebration, and many reception centers were organized for the American and English soldiers. Germaine, Kiko's sister, was in charge of one of them, and at about ten in the morning, going down the Rue Michelet, I stopped there for a moment. An atmosphere of somewhat artificial gaiety prevailed. Many of the soldiers were trying noisily to forget that they were going to spend Christmas far from home. I didn't like the false laughter, the sound of clinking glasses. I felt a need for calm and solitude. About eleven I settled in at the Coq Hardi, where a few comrades joined me.

I had not gone back to the Rue La Fayette. At heart I did not believe that Cordier's plan would be put into effect. I had the impression that it was a fine idea that would have no consequence, an Alexandre Dumas-like concept that would not materialize. Tomorrow, without doubt, Cordier would tell me, "We're going to organize the commando operation in the Rue Monge." Or else — why not — something altogether different would happen that would lead to a fortunate and unexpected solution. "Sit down in front of the door and wait. Someday you will see the corpse of your enemy float by in the current." What is more, you would have to get accustomed to waiting.

It was almost noon when I decided to go to lunch at Mont-Hydra. For several days my parents had scarcely seen me. I was moving toward the 302, which was parked opposite the brasserie in the Rue Balay, a little street that joined the Avenue Pasteur, when Jean-Bernard arrived.

"Come and have lunch with us at the Paris."

We passed my car. The Paris, at the corner of the Avenue Pasteur and the Boulevard Lafferrière, was close by. Jean-Bernard told me that Bonnier de la Chapelle was at the Summer Palace; Jean-Bernard had driven him there in an auto belonging to his father's office. At the Paris, we expected any minute the telephone call announcing that Darlan was dead.

We sat down at a small table, the only one free. Many of the people I had seen coming and going at the Rue La Fayette were there. We had lunch. Nothing happened. Louis Lalanne went to Henri d'Astier and spoke to him for a moment; then both came toward us.

"My dear Mario," said Henri d'Astier, "since you have a car handy, could you do our friend a service? He has no turkeys for his midnight celebration. There are some at Maison-Carrée, but he has no car; you would help him a lot if you could go and get them."

In other circumstances I would have found a way of avoiding the unpleasant task, but this time it was impossible. Henri d'Astier went back to his seat.

"Your father is obviously preoccupied," I observed to Jean-Bernard. "I have the impression that he let Lalanne bring up this story of his turkeys to be sure that our schedule was free this afternoon and that we were not participating in some action. Do you think he knows about Bonnier?"

"He may not even know how Cordier set things up. Anyway, I'm certain that he's unaware of Bonnier's role. He would certainly not have approved."

Jean-Bernard and I were getting ready to leave the restaurant to see about the turkeys when we saw Cordier get up from Henri d'Astier's table and go toward the double door, which was half open.

"It's Bonnier," said Jean-Bernard, who could see the street from his seat. He got up and went out after Cordier, returning quickly. "Darlan didn't come. Bonnier couldn't do anything. Cordier wants to see you."

Cordier seemed troubled and confused."Bonnier is going back to the

Summer Palace. He recognized your car and wants you to take him there, but he wants to try out his gun first. He's waiting for you by your car."

Jean-Bernard and I went toward the Rue Balay. Now I no longer asked myself any questions. Bonnier de la Chapelle was waiting, leaning on the car. He was a tall, handsome fellow, holding an umbrella. We shook hands as Jean-Bernard introduced us, and Bonnier said he knew me, as well as my 302, by sight. We opened the doors to climb in. Across the Rue Michelet, on the terrace of the Coq Hardi, five or six of our comrades, among them Roger, Kiko, André, saw us and came over. They all wanted to go with us, but I told them there was no room. Meanwhile Roger and Bonnier had shaken hands and seated themselves in the back seat of the Peugeot. Jean-Bernard got in beside me.

From the terrace of the Coq Hardi some 60 people watched us pass. Half of them knew or suspected what we were going to do. There were also a few policemen, who had been spying on us for several weeks.

Bonnier was absolutely calm, at ease. From time to time he exchanged a few words with Roger, showing no excitement or any other emotion. We might have been going to play tennis; he would have been no different.

We passed in front of the Summer Palace and continued on toward Hydra, where I turned off on an empty side road bordered with olive trees, near an old golf course. Bonnier lowered his window; he took out an enormous revolver and fired it. The first shot failed; the second and third went off properly. He asked if we had a more reliable weapon, and Jean-Bernard handed him the Rubis 7.65 that I had given him yesterday. Bonnier fired several shots: the pistol worked perfectly. Without saying a word, he put it into his pocket and gave the big revolver to Jean-Bernard, who placed it in the glove compartment. As we drove off, Bonnier asked me if I could furnish him with two full magazines. I had some at Mont-Hydra, less than 500 meters away, so we went there. When I stopped at the entrance to the garages, Bonnier said he would like a needle and some thread to sew up his trouser pocket: he didn't want to risk losing the magazines. I went up to my room, took two magazines out of a drawer and filled them with cartridges, then went to see my parents. My father was reading, and my mother happened to be sewing. I asked her for a needle and some strong thread and went back to the car, where Bonnier set about calmly sewing his pocket.

We drove in silence back to the Summer Palace. I stopped at the little church square at the entrance to the iron gate, where, in addition to the Mobile Guards, a tank had taken up its position. An attack was expected.

Bonnier got out of the car and told us not to park. He said goodbye and moved toward the gate. Regretfully, our hearts heavy, we left.

On the way I dropped Jean-Bernard off at the entrance to the Rue La Fayette so that he could bring Cordier up to date; then Roger and I picked up Kiko at the Coq Hardi and went after the turkeys. The traffic was heavy as I wove my way among the jeeps, the G.M.C.'s, and the carts. We were in a hurry to be done with this ridiculous inconvenience. When we got to Maison-Carrée, we found that there were no more turkeys. Back in Algiers, I left Roger and Kiko at the bottom of the Rue Michelet, stopped in at the Paris to tell Lalanne about the shortage of turkeys, then went back to the Rue La Fayette.

Madame d'Astier and her daughters were alone in the apartment, but scarcely had I arrived when someone rang the doorbell. It was Pose, out of breath. "Darlan is dead!" he announced.

Pose left, and Madame d'Astier asked me to take her and her daughters to the Saint-Augustin church, to pray. We started out, but after a few hundred meters the right rear tire of my Peugeot burst. My spare tire was unusable, so Madame d'Astier said she and her daughters would continue on foot. I looked for a garage, but it was the day before a holiday, and tires, even worn ones, had been hard to come by for a long time. Finally a dealer I knew promised me one for the next morning.

It was dark when I got back to the Rue La Fayette, where Jean-Bernard opened the door. Henri d'Astier and Cordier were there, with two or three others. Very serious news had just arrived. Bonnier, who had been unable to escape through the window as planned, had been taken not to the DST but to the judicial police, a building next to police headquarters. The judicial police and police headquarters were already filled with Mobile Guards. Bonnier had been recognized by a friend of his father; both were newspapermen at the *Echo d'Alger*.

"Why, it's Bonnier's son!" this journalist had cried out on seeing him get out of the police car.

So our friend was being detained in a heavily guarded place in which we had no accomplices, and his identity was known. Cordier told me to wait; he might need me.

Toward eight o'clock we had to return to the Paris, where Lalanne had absolutely insisted on inviting us to his Christmas Eve dinner. It was a strange atmosphere, where people we didn't know offered us champagne and invited us to drink a toast to celebrate Darlan's death. We got away as soon as we could.

At the Rue La Fayette, on that Christmas Eve, numerous visitors came in one after the other, walking through the hall into the dining room where Henri d'Astier stayed. Jean-Bernard and I kept to ourselves in a little room near the entrance, with the door closed. From time to time we heard the voices of Pose, Pierre Alexandre, and Marc Jacquet. Cordier came in, again asked us to wait, then left the door half open as he went out. The voice of Henri d'Astier reached us distinctly: "Above all, we must save this young man."

Cordier went to see Achiary at the DST but came back shortly: Achiary had no control over the judicial police.

To deprive him of any chance to escape with the help of accomplices, Bonnier de la Chapelle had been stripped of his clothes. Henri d'Astier and Bonnier were the same size, so Cordier went off to Achiary with one of Henri d'Astier's two suits, to try to organize an escape.

The front door opened and closed frequently. Below, autos drove off, came and went, most of the time between the Rue La Fayette and the Algéria. Cordier came to sit with us for a few minutes, to tell us briefly what had happened at the Summer Palace.

Before Bonnier had left with us in the Peugeot, Cordier had warned him not to claim to have an appointment with La Tour du Pin, who was actually at the Summer Palace, but to say that he was supposed to meet Louis Joxe, who would not be there. At first, everything took place as planned. Bonnier waited for the arrival of Darlan, then struck him down with two pistol shots as he was about to go into his office. Unfortunately, Captain Hourcade, Darlan's aide de camp, did not lose his sangfroid. He rushed at Bonnier and seized him by the throat and wrist. To get loose, Bonnier shot him in the leg; then he tried to run toward the window, which, as agreed, was open. But Hourcade's interference had given the guards time to run in, and they threw Bonnier to the floor, wounding him slightly in the face. One of them aimed his machine gun at him; if La Tour du Pin had not intervened, they would have killed him. In the uproar, no one paid attention to what Saint-Hardouin was saying, and Bonnier was led off to the judicial police.

It was absolutely necessary that the Count of Paris be invested by the

Council of the Empire very soon. Everything would come out all right if we were the ones to lead the inquiry.

Jean-Bernard and I asked Cordier if Darlan was killed immediately.

"He died almost at once, " he answered, "probably in the car transporting him to the Maillot Hospital or very soon afterward on the operating table."

"And what is the Count of Paris doing now?"

"This afternoon he came here after Marc Jacquet went to inform him at Sidi-Ferruch. He is now in the drawing room at the Hôtel Aletti, and Henri has just come back from there. The prince declared that he could not consider being raised to the presidency of the Council of Empire by illegal methods. A fine time to talk of legality! What else could we have tried? We don't have the means to attack in force. It's not the 18th Brumaire; and American tanks are roaming the streets of Algiers."

Alfred Pose appeared at the door of the dining room and asked Cordier to join him. The abbé left us, saying that he would let us know as soon as anything new came up.

Late at night, Henri d'Astier and some friends went to see Murphy. They had decided to present him with the possibility of arbitration by the Count of Paris, and to give up the idea of confronting the Americans with a fait accompli. The formalities of acknowledging the power vacuum and designating an interim government by the general councils would last several days. That would be too long. Only Murphy could establish a new government in time to save Bonnier.

Jean-Bernard and I remained alone. Madame d'Astier joined us, warmed up a cup of tea for us, then returned to her room. I was sure that, with her daughters, she was spending the night in prayer. We went down to the Boulevard Saint-Saëns. The American troops were on the alert, their tanks stationed at crossroads; and, to hide the city from Axis aircraft, batteries of smoke machines on the heights were covering it with a layer of artificial mist that gave the streets an unreal appearance. Now and then antiaircraft fire thundered and crackled over the bay. We went as far as the Boulevard Baudin, but access to the buildings of the judicial police was barred by a triple cordon of Mobile Guards. We returned to the Rue La Fayette and sat waiting in anxious silence, with two or three friends, to hear news of d'Astier's efforts to get someone to intervene.

A little before dawn Henri d'Astier and Cordier returned and shut themselves up in the dining room with some other men, and once more

Jean-Bernard and I were alone. Soon Cordier came to join us. Murphy had refused. He could not make the decision to enthrone the Count of Paris: that would be for the French people to decide when they could. For the moment, Murphy believed that he had to oppose any solution of this kind. Giraud, who had just gone to the Tunisian theater of operations, was urgently recalled, and there was every indication that he would be the one to succeed Darlan. Until his return, Noguès, then in Morocco, would be the interim appointee.

It had been a desperate attempt that had absolutely no chance of succeeding. Murphy had no desire to give unity to French factions whose division left the field free to him. His attitude showed that he had little doubt about the origin of the coup that had deprived him of so practical a man. We could expect no help from him to save Bonnier.

The execution of Bonnier was in the hands of Noguès and Bergeret. They would certainly do nothing definitive without Giraud, who would not get to Algiers until early afternoon. I proposed going to Cape Matifou to raise volunteers for an eventual attack in force against the judicial police. Everybody was in agreement, so I left with Jean-Bernard to see about the repairs to the 302. I finally found a tire, and at about ten o'clock I left Jean-Bernard at the Rue La Fayette, where they might need him, and sped off to the Demangeat farm.

On this Christmas day few people were there. New contingents had been sent to Bordj-bou-Arréridj, and I couldn't find Sabatier, who was almost never away. Almost everyone who was there was a stranger to me, but some I knew. They would assemble as many volunteers as possible and await instructions.

Back at the Rue La Fayette, I found that Jean-Bernard had gone to reconnoiter around the judicial police and central police headquarters. The Mobile Guards were still there in strength, with many of their officers. To take the site we would need the support of tanks, which we did not have. Nevertheless we were ready for anything.

The press, with enormous headlines, had announced the event. Not a word about Bonnier. The act was attributed to an Axis fanatic who wanted to punish Darlan for being a turncoat.

I went for lunch at my grandmother's on the Boulevard Lafferrière for the traditional Christmas turkey. My father, his brow furrowed with anxiety, took me aside.

"It was you, wasn't it?"

In a few sentences I told him everything. He was overwhelmed. "And this young man. He is done for?"

"We are trying to save him."

"All of you are done for."

The luncheon ended; I could go back to the Rue La Fayette. I had been there for only a few minutes when someone I didn't know came to announce that Giraud had arrived at the Summer Palace.

"Can you drive me to the Summer Palace?" Henri d'Astier asked me. It was Christmas; his chauffeur had the day off.

We left in the 302. He showed his card at the main gate, and the guards opened up. I drove through the gardens to the arcades at the entrance to the palace, where Henri d'Astier went on in.

I waited in the car for a half-hour, perhaps more. I observed idly that it was lucky that the Mobile Guards were not the same as yesterday. I would not have been surprised to see them burst out suddenly and surround the car, but this idea left me indifferent: in any case, they would not bring Darlan back to life. Henri d'Astier came back, more relaxed.

"I told Giraud that I took entire responsibility for everything," he told me. "At the end he assured me, 'Don't worry; I will do nothing for the moment.'"

Hope returned that all of it might yet make some sense. It was possible, now that Darlan was dead, that Giraud would turn out to be the leader we hoped for. He could easily save Bonnier. Fate was going to smile on us at last. After leaving Henri d'Astier at the Rue La Fayette, I returned to Cape Matifou to give those who were there instructions to wait.

The next morning, December 26, toward 8:30, I rang at the Rue La Fayette. Arlette, in tears, opened the door. Madame d'Astier, Eliane, and Marie-Béatrice were sitting, weeping, in the dining room. Bonnier de la Chapelle had been shot that morning. Our hope of yesterday had been a cheat. Bonnier had died alone.

Jean-Bernard told me what had happened during the night. At about eight, Alfred Pose and other friends had brought alarming news to the Rue La Fayette. Giraud was completely under the control of Noguès and Bergeret, who urged him to make an example by executing Bonnier in order to discourage new attacks. If Darlan was killed, they would be killed

too. They had to strike hard immediately. The military court immediately
went ahead with the formality of a verdict. Bonnier was condemned to
death, the sentence to be executed at once.

While the hours passed inexorably, a fierce struggle had gone on. More
than a hundred Mobile Guards defended the approaches to the military
tribunal on the Rue Cavaignac, where Bonnier de la Chapelle, once more
deprived of his clothing, was detained after sentencing. Neither Achiary
nor any of the inspectors succeeded in reaching him to give him Henri
d'Astier's suit or to try to help him escape. It was impossible in so short a
time to assemble sufficient forces to launch an assault, which, in any case,
would have run the risk of bringing about the immediate execution of the
condemned man. All night long, Henri d'Astier, Alfred Pose, Louis Joxe,
Jacques de Saint-Hardouin, La Tour du Pin, Marc Jacquet, Bret, the director of *France Presse*, doubled their efforts to influence Noguès, who had
just arrived from Morocco, then Giraud, then Bergeret.

At the Algéria and at the Rue La Fayette, where Cordier was coordinating all the efforts, the telephone was used desperately, without concern
for the bugging that recorded all conversations. Captain Beaufre, Giraud's
aide de camp, tried several times to make his chief yield somewhat.
Jacques de Saint-Hardouin went to see Murphy, who refused categori-
cally to intervene in favor of Bonnier.

"President Roosevelt has rigorously condemned this murder," said the
consul. "It is not for the Americans to take a position against a French
court-martial. It is a crime to have killed Darlan."

"Then you are the criminal," declared Saint-Hardouin. "You imposed
him, you condemned him to death."

It was Noguès who, according to instructions left by Darlan, held power
in the interim until the designation of a high commissioner by the Council of the Empire. Bonnier de la Chapelle's pardon therefore depended on
him. He put the decision into the hands of Giraud, whom he already considered to be tacitly designated for the succession. The Vichyites and Murphy were in agreement in thinking that Giraud as high commissioner
would be the most convenient screen to allow everything to continue as
before.

Giraud refused the pardon. On the telephone at the Rue La Fayette,
Alfred Pose then threatened the officials of Darlan's cabinet with terrible
reprisals and an impossible life for Giraud if the sentence were to be carried out.

"Tell your friends that we have a list of 20 or 30 people to lock up so that we won't be bothered," was the answer.

At the end of this night of bitterness and anguish, while the alerts and air raids over Algiers succeeded each other in the rumbling of ack-ack guns, the attempts to save Bonnier gradually proved to be hopeless. As dawn was beginning to break, Henri d'Astier and Alfred Pose again went to Giraud for one final attempt.

"We are applying the law of an eye for an eye; he has killed, he will be killed," the general told them stubbornly, in a curt, dismissive tone, for once sure of himself. It was he who finally gave the written order to proceed with the execution at the time planned.

Thus he had executed one of those who opened wide the gates of Algiers to him, the one who had just freed him from the infamous association that he had accepted and which subordinated him to a double traitor. It would have been so simple for him to wait for the end of the war for Bonnier de la Chapelle to be judged by a tribunal created by a legal government. He fell into the crude trap of Noguès and Bergeret, and now he was tied to them.

Seated in the dining room, Madame d'Astier and her daughters wept in silence. Through the windows came the echoes of a military band, of parades, of the rolling of drums. It was the grandiose funeral procession of Darlan.

Jean-Bernard reported that his father was at that moment at the office of Master Sansonetti, the lawyer who, last night, was Bonnier's defender. In the afternoon I went to see Sansonetti, on the Rue Rovigo. His eyes red, still overcome, he told me about the last moments of Bonnier de la Chapelle.

"I could do nothing, absolutely nothing; everything was settled ahead of time. The coffin was already prepared before the sentence. My protests went unheard. With courage and admirable calm, this 20-year-old declared, 'I have brought to justice a traitor who prevented the union of all Frenchmen.' I was able to accompany him to the firing range at Hussein-dey, where the execution took place. While he was praying, the officer gave the order to fire. He is buried in his family's tomb in the cemetery of Saint-Eugène. His act was necessary; he took it upon himself and sacrificed himself for all of us. I bow before him; to do what he did required something more than courage, more than submission."

Epilogue

GIRAUD BECAME HIGH COMMISSIONER. The Council of the Empire, composed of himself, Noguès, Bergeret, Boisson, and Chatel, elected him unanimously. Roosevelt and Murphy had time to appreciate the lack of character, the mediocrity of the man, who was perhaps an even more pragmatic choice than Darlan: he accepted the succession completely passively and did not carry with him a loaded past. Giraud's immediate entourage consisted of Noguès and Bergeret. No one questioned the validity of the Darlan-Clark accords or attempted to bring up again those between Giraud and Murphy.

The attempt by the Count of Paris to arbitrate failed, and it was impossible to present Murphy with a fait accompli. In fact, those who had tried to force his hand had to appear before him as beggars in the attempt to save Bonnier. According to Roosevelt's instructions, Murphy allowed Bonnier to be shot to demonstrate the noninterference of Americans in French affairs; then he had the Council of the Empire enthrone the one who suited them best. Most of those who had given their approval to the possibility of arbitration by the prince went back into their shells when they observed the solidity of the American opposition. Many had prudently withdrawn when they learned that the man who had assassinated the admiral was under arrest and that his identity was known. In the hours before the election of the new high commissioner, the repeated offers by the Count of Paris to become a candidate encountered polite refusals everywhere. Now that the deed was done, why risk the appearance of having been an accomplice?

On the morning of the execution of Bonnier de la Chapelle, the Count of Paris, accompanied by Alfred Pose, had been received by Giraud at the Villa Monfeld. While the prince was asking for a pardon for the condemned man, the general himself informed him that "the assassin of the admiral" had just been executed. After a long silence, the Count of Paris explained to him that, in addition to the military problems, there were also political problems of great importance to be solved; that he, Giraud, could not be a unifying force, and that it would be necessary to involve Gaullist elements in the rebuilding of France.

Giraud, incapable of understanding the complex reality of the situation in North Africa, answered, "I am going to be designated to succeed Admiral Darlan. I am a profound monarchist, but my duty is to accept this post. My Lord, it is not possible for you to occupy the seat of the president, for it is stained with blood."

In a few hours the prince had to acknowledge that all he had left as supporters were the few loyal companions who had organized his coming to Algiers. A few true friends, who could do nothing more.

Meanwhile, at the Summer Palace the members of the junta were afraid of us. They feared to be shot down according to a list drawn up by order of position and urgency. Giraud, completely conditioned by Bergeret, thought he would be the first victim. We did not know if he had told those around him about his interview of December 25 with Henri d'Astier; but, no doubt feeling himself more guilty than they because of his failure to keep his word, he was overcome with panic and never left the Summer Palace unless hidden in a shabby civilian car. For the moment, only the fear of unleashing acts of reprisal prevented the group from doing anything. They were preparing to "pulverize" us.

Henri d'Astier was invited to give up his functions as assistant secretary of the Interior, but he remained at the Chantiers de la Jeunesse as an assistant to Van Hecke, whose solidarity with us was totally reliable.

The apartment in the Rue La Fayette was quiet and sad. Everybody avoided useless meetings, discreetly passing on the intelligence that arrived through intermediaries from the Summer Palace, where Henri d'Astier still had intelligence sources. Cordier seldom left, and I often stayed for lunch. Bitter words were never spoken. We were waiting.

Once I found myself alone with Cordier, when Jean-Bernard had gone out with his mother and sisters and Henri d'Astier had gone to 16 Rue Michelet to meet Jacques Brunel. The abbé was seated on the couch in the entrance hall, deeply sad, lost in thought. To break the silence, I asked him why Bergeret exhibited an attitude so harsh and hostile to us, whereas he had earlier placed himself at the orders of the Count of Paris. As though he were speaking of a subject that no longer concerned him, Cordier answered me:

"Bergeret has made considerable progress. Before giving in to Murphy by voting for Giraud, he presented the prince's candidacy to the Council of the Empire. He doesn't want to give any impression of being responsible, now, for the murder of Darlan. If everything had gone according to the original plan, if the claim that it was an Axis agent had been believed, I think things would have been quite different. It's not the reality that frightens them, it's that what really happened might become known. We lost the game when Bonnier was taken away to the office of the judicial police and when he was recognized. Now our fate will depend on what becomes public, what is revealed. To the extent that what we did becomes more evident, Giraud and Bergeret will attack us all the more, to prove their innocence, to avoid being contaminated. I learned yesterday that an official of the judicial police, Commissioner Garidacci, was able to get to Bonnier in the hours preceding the execution. He offered to help him, to get in touch with whatever friends he might have. Bonnier told him a few secrets. For the moment Garidacci has done no more than let me know. He's staying quiet, hoping to profit by his silence. But a few days from now, when he perceives that we no longer count, he'll be tempted to improve his standing with those in authority. But it's all unimportant. Everything is finished now."

My parents had nothing to say in defense of Darlan. The execution of Bonnier made them indignant, and their scorn for Giraud was intense. Now I was going home earlier in the evening, and I often sensed my mother's warm glance resting on me. Since the age of two she had been an invalid. Her childhood and adolescence were spent in clinics, or at Berck in one of those long narrow baby carriages in which children who cannot walk are taken for a ride. I kissed her and said gently to her, "Don't worry."

Roger and Kiko thought they could join the Free Corps at Bordj-bou-Arréridj. Rumor had it that the first contingents were going to be moved toward Tunisia. As for me, it was no longer possible. At Cape Matifou, Gilbert Sabatier, who had noticed the disappearance of his Colt on the morning of the 25th, doubtless thought he was doing the right thing by immediately going to the military police. He was now locked up in the military prison at the Pélissier barracks. Squadrons of Mobile Guards occupied the camp and asked where I was. The military police, who were watching the farm, were to be notified without delay if I came there. They did not appear to be looking for me elsewhere; it was presumably a local measure that must have been the result of my visits to the camp on the 25th. I avoided showing myself at the Rue Charras; there was no point in compromising my comrades.

On the 26th, Roger had shown me photos that Bonnier had given him when we were in the 302. Identity photos, handsome and expressive, taken no doubt on December 22 for the false identity card and passport. I asked Roger now for one of these photos, but his father had found them and burned them.

As I was going along the Rue Michelet in the Peugeot, I saw Denise walking toward the trolley bus. I stopped opposite her. "Well begun, badly ended," she said on getting into the car.

On the Rue d'Isly, when I was walking toward the Etoile to have lunch with Daridan, I met Germain Libine. "How did you get involved in an affair so badly organized? It's even worse than when Colette shot at Laval." [In 1941 Paul Colette wounded Laval during a parade at Versailles.]

"You should have done it yourself, since you're so capable!"

"I'm shooting off at the mouth because I'm worried about you. Your skin is worth more than the 12 bullets you're going to get. You must disappear from sight for a long time."

"No."

"You want to give them this pleasure?

"I don't give a damn."

In the Rue Michelet I came upon Edmond Benhamou. He was even more caustic. "Well, Mario, I didn't know you were a royalist! Here I was, thinking you were a Gaullist."

I didn't answer, but more and more I thought that, by good luck or by Machiavellianism, de Gaulle had killed two birds with one stone.

When I reached the Rue La Fayette, Henri d'Astier and Cordier were at that very moment talking about de Gaulle. I asked them whether they didn't think it would be he who would win the prize in the end. Sad and composed, Henri d'Astier answered me.

"That's what I was telling the abbé. Here's de Gaulle, free of the two real obstacles to his assuming power in Algeria. First Darlan, who would have refused to the end to yield his place, then the Count of Paris, whom he could not have outranked if our plan had succeeded. De Gaulle has made use of one to strike down the other. The Count of Paris caused Darlan to disappear, but, right here in Algiers and too closely connected to the action, he eliminated himself at the same time. As it's impossible for us to reveal the truth without betraying the fundamental interests of our country's unity and the struggle against the occupier, the man in London now has a clear road. Time is working for him. As early as December 25 he was declaring officially that the murder of Darlan was a deplorable crime, but at the same time he was sending a telegram to Giraud. We know the terms of this message: 'The assassination at Algiers is an indication and a warning. An indication of the exasperation into which the tragedy of France has thrown the mind and soul of the French people. A warning of the consequences of the absence of a national authority. It is more than ever necessary that this national unity be established. I propose that you meet me as soon as possible in order to study ways to group all French forces under a provisional authority.' As you can see, de Gaulle hasn't lost any time. We can understand that Giraud feels himself to be under attack, all the more so since, through indiscretions, he has learned about the directive received by the Gaullist leaders of Algiers at the very moment that de Gaulle was making this offer, which seems like an ultimatum. On the 25th, during the evening program, Radio London broadcast this message for Algiers: 'Buy a red donkey.' According to the codes that my brother gave Capitant, that means, 'Liberty of action against Giraud.' A few more tricks like this and all de Gaulle will have to do is seize power without sharing it and without supervision. That is exactly what we wanted to avoid."

"What else could we do?" I asked him.

"We had to obey. To refuse to carry out that order was to confirm everything we've been fighting against and cut us off from the Resistance in metropolitan France — in a word, to betray our cause. Around December 10 they considered sending my brother Emmanuel to establish a liaison with Algiers. But Emmanuel refused. After a few days in London, he was supposed to be taken back to France at night by an English plane. A visit to Algiers would have completely discredited him with his companions in the struggle. A leader of the Resistance could not risk the impression that he had come to pledge allegiance to Darlan. That's why it was François who came. And if my brother agreed to convey de Gaulle's message, 'Darlan must disappear,' it was because certain words of de Gaulle had clearly led him to understand that if he, de Gaulle, could not arrive in Algiers under the conditions he was asking for, he was ready to go to Moscow in order to be near those who would become the masters of the game. In order to save what could still be saved, he said. So, at least we have achieved one thing. De Gaulle will be able to arrive from the west, which is preferable, after all."

Cordier intervened. "That's right, but if my plan had worked all the way, in the first place Bonnier would be alive, which would count most, but also we would have succeeded in carrying out our mission without pulling the chestnuts out of the fire for de Gaulle. The execution of Darlan attributed to an Axis agent was the only solution for a true reconciliation."

"Maybe it was the only way that would let us both execute the order and pursue our projects," answered d'Astier. "De Gaulle would certainly have been disappointed if we had achieved our ends. He would have had to be satisfied with second place. But what good is it to go over all that? In addition to our sorrow, we have to accept this lesson in humility. Perhaps the success of November 8 made us too sure of ourselves. So we'll suffer the consequences of our failure. We played our role for the Resistance in metropolitan France, and that's probably all that matters. In spite of everything, I hope I will be able to fight the Boche again. That's now my only wish."

In the Peugeot going up toward Hydra under a dark sky, I thought, "It's lucky there are still the Boche. If they are the cause, at least in some circumstances they can become the solution."

One afternoon my father paid a visit to Henri d'Astier. I was there, and we all sat down together. I took the initiative: "I know you want to reproach Henri d'Astier for having dragged me into this questionable adventure — although you know perfectly well that I never do anything I don't want to do! As I see it, two things have been achieved: the landing succeeded, and Darlan is dead. As far as I'm concerned, what happens next doesn't matter."

"What are you going to do now?" my father asked d'Astier.

"We can't do anything."

My father expressed his wish that from now on I should live completely at the Rue La Fayette, to remain under the continuous protection of Henri d'Astier. In this way, he reasoned, anyone would think twice before arresting me. We agreed immediately. So much the better if my father still had the illusion that Henri d'Astier could protect me.

That evening, when we were going to bed, Cordier absolutely refused either the cushions or the springs that he and Jean-Bernard usually shared. Jean-Bernard slept on the springs, I was on the cushions, and Cordier spent the night stretched out on the tile floor.

The next day Roger, Kiko, and I installed ourselves at 38 Rue Michelet at the home of friends of the Rosfelders, the Trapps. Like other people in Algiers who owned a farm in the interior, they had retreated there to spend their nights without being disturbed by air raids. We slept there in absolute tranquillity, our three pistols placed on the bureau. At each alert during the night we could hear the inhabitants of the building scrambling down the stairs to take refuge in the cellar. The ack-ack thundered; a few bombs fell in the distance. We felt like strangers to all of it.

Intelligence that came to Henri d'Astier indicated that Bergeret, to whom Giraud had abandoned all authority, was hesitating only over the best way to strike at us. He was trying to assess our ability to respond; he was unaware so far of our weakness. At Cape Matifou our armament was seized by the gendarmerie, and the military police returned to ask about us. Roger and Kiko were waiting from one day to the next for their departure for Bordj-bou-Arréridj.

A friend of the Rosfelders, Air Force Lieutenant Réginensi, and other aviator friends offered to try to help us reach one of the regions of Africa held by the Free French forces. We refused; the people at the Summer Palace would be only too happy.

Henri d'Astier decided it was necessary to regularize my military situation. The Chantiers de la Jeunesse had been militarized and Van Hecke had resumed his rank of colonel. We went to see him at his La Robertsau headquarters on the heights of Algiers. I was attached to his secretariat as a noncommissioned officer.

"You will schedule your own time," Van Hecke told me.

There I was in uniform, transferred in proper form from the Free Corps, so I could not be accused of desertion. Beginning the next morning, I sorted papers behind a desk, in the company of an adjutant.

On the morning of December 30, when I arrived at La Robertsau, Van Hecke informed me that almost all of our friends had been arrested. In the night, the Mobile Guards, carrying tommy guns and grenades, forced their way into the different homes, breaking down the doors. In handcuffs, André Achiary, Jacques Brunel, José Aboulker, Professor Henri Aboulker, Raphaël, Pierre Alexandre, André Temime, police officials Esquerré, Bringuard, Muscatelli, and more than 20 others were taken to an unknown destination.

During the day we learned that it was Bergeret who had organized the operation. The evidence indicated that he was seeking to decapitate Henri d'Astier's general staff and deprive him of his supporters. The list had been made up somewhat at random, using the names of the principal actors in the landing operations. Murphy did not react. Since November 8, his policy had now turned around to such a degree that he had allowed Vichyite leaders to arrest en masse the members of the Algerian Resistance. The PPF and the SOL were jubilant, boasting openly that they were getting organized to finish us off.

At the Rue La Fayette, we were warned that the junta of the Summer Palace would now watch the reactions of Henri d'Astier in order to take the necessary measures before striking at the leader. As d'Astier had no means of organizing an effective response, the outcome was near.

Henri d'Astier concealed under his customary self-control the deep sorrow that he had felt since December 26. "Some of them can't resist the temptation of taking revenge for the humiliation of November 8, but these people have yielded above all to their fear," he observed. "They are frightened for their lives, quite simply. Without being certain, they now have an idea where the coup originated."

I completed the thought. "They're telling themselves that if a few more of them are executed, de Gaulle will only have to land peacefully at the Maison-Blanche airport."

"They should have thought of that sooner," continued d'Astier. "They weren't smart enough to accept the arbitration of the Count, so they have missed their last chance. In these next weeks, just when Hitler, who's stuck in the icy plains of Russia, begins his decline, Noguès, Bergeret, and their zealots are going to look like the agents of a great error: collaboration with an enemy who's going to lose the war. As for Giraud, just out of captivity, he's found himself mixed up in problems that are beyond him. He's beginning to understand. Pose just told me that he regrets having agreed to these arrests. For the moment he has refused to allow Cordier and me to be part of the prize. The others have agreed to wait, no doubt expecting to isolate us and to put us in a dubious light with respect to our friends. But for Giraud it's too late. On the night of December 25, when he was giving a definitive and absolute refusal to Beaufre's attempt to save Bonnier, he said, 'This affair doesn't burn any bridges.' Well, now he has burned his bridges and lined up beside those who have already lost. In the wake of the coming victory it's de Gaulle who will rise to the top; Algiers cannot moderate his hegemony at all."

The next evening it was my turn for guard duty at La Robertsau. At midnight the sirens of all the boats in the harbor suddenly began to wail; the sky was afire with tracer shells from all the antiaircraft batteries. I had forgotten that it was the end of the year.

Roger and Kiko left for their unit of the Free Corps at Bordj-bou-Arréridj. I gave the Peugeot back to Dr. Alcay. Jean-Bernard, who had been going around for several days with a bad sore throat, had to be transported to Maillot Hospital, where he was fighting a high fever complicated by a serious attack of malaria. Daridan and Marcel Fellus insisted on putting me up for the night, but I preferred to go back to Mont-Hydra.

We knew that our friends who had been arrested were being detained at Laghouat, an oasis in the Southern Territories. Bernard Karsenty, who was with José when the gendarmes struck, managed to get away. He found asylum at the English consulate and was trying to provoke a response from the Allied command to help us.

At the Rue La Fayette there was still the same calm marked with sadness. Henri d'Astier displayed his usual control, trying not to speak of what was preoccupying us. We didn't even discuss what system of defense would be best against the interrogation that would soon come. Even if we wanted to, what good was it to argue? We knew that several people on the Avenue Pasteur had noticed Cordier's coming and going between the Paris café and Bonnier. Bonnier had gotten into the car in front of 60 spectators, among them some policemen. We had given him a weapon taken from a marine, with a number that was certainly on record. I had taken that gun to an armorer, who wrote down my identity and the number of the weapon. We had dropped Bonnier in front of the gate at the Summer Palace, under the eyes of the Mobile Guards, and he had presented a false identity card in the name of Morand, which could only have been provided by certain police services. Finally, a few days ago, an unknown person had accosted Henri d'Astier at the lower end of the Boulevard Saint-Saëns and offered him a piece of paper, saying, "This is the deposition of Kalfort and Leplan. I need 200,000 francs."

"I don't have that sum, and in any case I wouldn't give it to you. Do whatever you wish,' answered d'Astier.

Cordier had just put back on his uniform of lieutenant in Military Security; he had chosen to be arrested as a soldier. Never had the abbé alluded to the sacrifice that he had agreed to make for his country when he chose to be a resister. Modestly as usual, the priest within him had stepped aside. Now he had reached the end of his engagement; he had given more than his life. If he could survive, his would be a life of suffering, solitude, penitence.

On the evening of January 8, Cordier opened the door for me at the Rue La Fayette. "Garidacci has talked," he said.

Later, when we were alone, he asked, "Mario, do you think I would have given Bonnier the instructions that allowed him to act if I had thought for an instant that it would end this way?"

I answered that I knew that wasn't the case, that I had solidly approved of this action, and still did, that I shared the responsibility.

"Do you believe that I feel deeply that the death of Darlan was not worth the life of Bonnier?"

"Yes, we all think that. But nothing can be done over. We have to know how to accept. Even the worst."

We were silent for a moment; then he questioned me again. "Tell me, Mario. You really don't give a damn?"

"That's right."

He went toward the door, and I heard him murmur, "Thanks."

I said goodbye to Denise. She gave me a minuscule packet containing a little strand of her blond hair.

On January 10, as usual after leaving La Robertsau, I rang at the Rue La Fayette. An unknown person opened the door, a pistol in his hand, and in the corridor were other armed civilians. Madame d'Astier and her daughters were sitting silently in the dining room. In the semi-darkness I recognized several of these men; they were inspectors of the DST, among them Dominique Lentali. "We have to take you with us," he said.

I took leave of Madame d'Astier and the girls. Two inspectors, one of them Dominique, were at my side as we left for the DST. On the way I asked Lentali who had replaced Achiary as commissioner.

"It's Chief Inspector Loffredo."

"What's he like?"

"He's okay. His brother was killed by the Boche."

At the Italian House some Senegalese under European officers stood on guard with their bayonets fixed. The inspectors were armed with the Sten guns that we had given them.

Jo Loffredo sat behind his desk. He was very brown, muscular, looking like a corsair. At first glance, we liked each other, but we were both reserved.

"Why am I being arrested?"

"Monsieur Henri d'Astier and Abbé Cordier have been held since this morning in the military prison of the Pélissier barracks. We were ordered to set up a trap at his residence. You fell into it."

"What are you going to do?"

"For the moment no one has given me any special instructions concerning you. So, since it is not up to me to take the initiative in arresting you, you are free."

In that special tone that policemen have when discreetly giving advice, he added, "That's not going to last. See that you do what you have to do."

I left the Italian House and went to the Hydra trolley bus stop. In the evening crowd some friends hailed me. Having already heard about my arrest, they could not believe their eyes on seeing me free, and they offered to hide me. At Mont-Hydra I warned my parents that I would probably be arrested the next day. I asked them not to hold against me the worry I was causing them. They responded only with affection.

The next morning I went back to the Rue La Fayette. There were no inspectors, and without Henri d'Astier and Cordier the apartment seemed empty. Madame d'Astier and her daughters told me how the policemen had broken in, brandishing their guns. Arlette had opened the door. Henri d'Astier was shaving.

"Put your weapons away, you look ridiculous," he said to them and, paying no attention to them, he finished shaving.

I went back to Mont-Hydra for lunch, and my father reported that less than a quarter of an hour after my departure inspectors had come in two cars. They asked where they could find me. "It is very urgent," one of them had said.

After lunch I went back down to the city. I ran into Germain Libine, and we went to pay a visit to Guy Cohen in his Elysée Couture store. They both scolded me for not taking off. Ten minutes had not passed before two inspectors of the DST entered the store. They appeared relieved. The fact that they had let me go yesterday was not taken well in high places. Guy Cohen declared that they would never arrest me in his store, but I shook hands with Guy and Germain and left, escorted by the two agents. At the DST, Loffredo said it was lucky that his inspectors had found me. Since morning, everyone had been looking for me, and if the Mobile Guards had caught me they would have taken me to the judicial police, whereas here I had friends.

They left me in a sort of hallway that connected the offices on the third floor. A glass door opened onto the stair landing. In front of the door and on the landing were Senegalese infantrymen, and a few American MP's were also on guard. Originally they had been put there at Achiary's request as a reinforcement against a possible raid by the SOL, and now they had become my jailers.

Inspector Mattéi, one of Achiary's favorites, came out to talk to me. We knew each other well.

"Look at what we've come to," he said. "We are the ones who arrest you now. Today more than ever I wish I could turn in my badge. Tell me what I can do and I will do it."

I didn't need anything.

Others came to express their sympathy. We walked back and forth in the hallway or gathered to sit on scattered chairs. Paul Plantier, Schmitt, Mattéi, Henri Colonna recalled the year 1941, when as enthusiastic and loyal companions of Achiary they secretly tracked down Axis spies who were doing everything they could to speed up the Nazi seizure of North Africa.

Epic adventures, in the course of which many of these spies mysteriously disappeared. Finally the Vichy people became suspicious and dismantled the DST.

Mattéi informed me that the Count of Paris, at the urgent request of Giraud, had quietly returned to Morocco the previous day, accompanied by General Ronin. Since morning, Commissioner Garidacci had been imprisoned at the Pélissier barracks.

"Which proves," remarked Mattéi, "that he would have done better to hold his tongue."

After a while no one bothered about me. If I had had the least desire to do so, I could have walked calmly past the guards to the street. A little inspector with a squirrel-monkey face must have guessed my thoughts. He went over to the Senegalese and, pointing at me, said, "Watch out, he's in uniform but he's a prisoner. He's very dangerous." The guards aimed their bayonets at me with frightened looks.

Night fell. The glass door opened and Germain came in, face drawn. Where was the time when, only a few days ago, we felt at home at the DST, when Germain proudly pointed me out to the inspectors: "Twenty years old, gentlemen. Can you imagine?"

Germain addressed the policemen: "What are you going to do?"

"We don't know. We're waiting for orders."

"If anything happens to him, you'll be answerable to me."

"Believe me, we'll do nothing to him."

He left, but an hour later he looked into the room again. "Everything okay?"

Mattéi told him he would get me something to eat and set me up for the night. Germain left, and Mattéi brought me some *café au lait* and croissants. He installed me in a sort of storeroom that opened onto the hallway by a door with gray-painted glass windows. He went back to get a little radio, which he plugged in, and we placed some chairs side by side: to sleep, I would just stretch out on them. He went off, and I turned off the radio and lay down on the chairs. The lights of the hallway were on; there was quite a lot of light.

High up on the wall a transom opened up and a head appeared, belonging to a fellow of about 30. He called softly, "Hey, you!"

I didn't answer.

"You, old man. Are you okay?"

I stayed silent.

"Tell me, you. Did they give you an electric shock?"

He must have been an SOL or an Axis spy being held next door. After a minute I heard the transom close softly. I went to sleep.

The next morning Mattéi again brought me coffee and croissants. I could wash myself, and with some of the guards I went out on the balcony for a few minutes. When I passed in front of the Senegalese, who were not the same ones as last night, the inspector with the monkey face warned them, "Watch out. He's very dangerous."

The other inspectors rebuked him: "You ought to be ashamed."

"He's the worst member of the brigade," they told me by way of excuse.

They seemed to be waiting for authorities outside their service. I was confined to the room with the transom, and the glass door was shut, the guards posted in front of it. Loffredo and Mattéi came frequently to keep me company, and at the end of the morning my father arrived, accompanied by Germain. My father had been to the office of the barrister Colonna d'Ornano, a brother of the Colonel d'Ornano who was a companion of Leclerc and was killed at Koufra.

"He told me that he is personally too compromised to undertake your defense effectively."

"I don't want any lawyer. I don't see the need of it."

Taking advantage of a moment when we were alone together, my father told me, "Since last night we have received three telephone calls at Hydra. Two of the callers refused to give their names. The third was Captain Bouin. Each time it was a warning to be on guard, that there was a plan to provoke your escape and then to take advantage of it to shoot you down."

I reassured him. Mattéi joined us, and he, too, calmed my father down; then Germain and my father left.

Mealtime arrived. I was going to lunch with the most reputable detainees of the establishment. Mattéi brought me the list as though it were a social event. A dozen names: an architect, an engineer, two or three "young and pretty" women, one of them a princess who bore one of the oldest names in France. We went to their little refectory, where Loffredo introduced me: "One of my friends, who comes to share your table."

Each of them greeted me politely. The fellow in the transom was not one of the guests. We ate in silence.

At two, Loffredo announced that I was to be taken to the judicial police on the Rue Cavaignac, to a military court, for interrogation by an examining magistrate. He accompanied me to the landing and wished me good luck. With three policemen, one of them Dominique Lentali, I got into the car, and when we arrived one of the inspectors said, "We didn't want to handcuff you, but if you try anything we will be obliged to shoot."

I did not answer. Dominique let me know, in a somewhat comical pantomime, that if I wanted to escape, he would help me, but I signaled to him that I would not try.

The entry hall of the military tribunal was teeming with Mobile Guards. Dominique reported that the judge who was going to interrogate me was Major Voituriez, and the head of the military court was Colonel Laroubine. They had arrived from Morocco a few days earlier.

The door of the judge's office opened, and Van Hecke came out, greeting me. "My dear Mario, do you know that Henri is only being accused of complicity in an assassination?" We shook hands.

I was led into the interrogation room. It was barely furnished and badly lighted. Standing near his desk a major was waiting, while behind another smaller desk was another officer, the clerk. Voituriez was rather tall, with a commanding bearing and a penetrating glance. He sat down, signaled for me to sit facing him, and then quickly stood up again. In a crisp, severe tone he began:

"You are here because a crime has been committed. A man is dead and the perpetrator of this assassination has already paid for his deed. We are looking for other criminals, as guilty as he, so that they may receive in their turn the punishment they deserve."

He looked at me to see what effect he had produced. Apparently none. Suddenly I didn't want this man to win. It was essential that I manage to find out how much he knew.

"You don't kill a man because you no longer want him," Voituriez continued. "I am the first to recognize that it was necessary for Admiral Darlan to go. It would have sufficed to wait. He would have left of his own accord."

"That is quite right."

"What! You say it is quite right?"

"Yes."

"And nevertheless you contributed to this murder. You are even the most direct accomplice of Fernand Bonnier de la Chapelle."

"I still wonder if it was really Bonnier de la Chapelle who killed Admiral Darlan."

"What?"

"Yes, I can't accept it. It sometimes seems unbelievable to me."

He was baffled. "What are you saying?"

"I can't help thinking it's a plot."

"We have many witnesses who saw you take Bonnier de la Chapelle to the Summer Palace in your car, and you say he was not the one?"

"I'm not saying he wasn't the one, but that I have trouble believing he was."

"What do you mean? You do not deny having transported him to the scene of the crime?"

"No, not at all."

"Therefore you acknowledge it."

"Certainly I admit that I took Bonnier de la Chapelle to the summer Palace, but I don't see . . ."

Now, if he had other charges, he would not be able to restrain himself from leveling them at me.

"Well then, it is clear to you. What more do you need? Do you want to read the depositions of the witnesses?"

"What could they say?"

"Come now. That they were present at the scene of your departure with Bonnier de la Chapelle!"

It seemed to me that there were no other witness statements. I tried again. "When you cut me off, I was going to tell you that I did, in fact, take Bonnier as far as the Summer Palace, but he simply said that he had an appointment. My comrades and I were unaware of his intentions."

"That is astonishing. You tell me you did not know that Bonnier de la Chapelle was going to kill Darlan?"

"Absolutely."

"So, according to you, he said nothing to you about it? He is your friend, he is going to commit such an act, you take him to the scene of the crime, and you know nothing about it?"

"I did not know Bonnier de la Chapelle. I saw him for the first time when he asked me, as I was getting into my car, whether I was going in the direction of the Summer Palace."

"But he knew you?"

"By sight. We had friends in common at the Free Corps. He recognized my car, which he had noticed at Cape Matifou."

"Did he know Jean-Bernard d'Astier and Rosfelder?"

"When Jean-Bernard, Rosfelder, and I got to the car, we saw that

Bonnier was waiting. Rosfelder was in the Chantiers de la Jeunesse with him; he recognized him, introduced us; and, as I said that we were going to Hydra to see my parents before going to Maison-Carrée to get some turkeys, Bonnier asked me to drop him off at the Summer Palace."

Voituriez appeared to have lost his breath. "To get turkeys!" he gasped.

"An errand for a friend."

"And you noticed nothing abnormal in the attitude of Bonnier de la Chapelle? He was going to commit murder. In the car, you doubtless discussed the weather?"

"That's what I was telling you just now. Bonnier was so calm, so natural, that when we learned of the death of Admiral Darlan we could not believe that he was the one who fired."

"When you heard about it, what did you do then?"

"We were very concerned. We agreed to keep still about this whole affair."

Up to now Voituriez had been walking up and down the room, waving his arms. Suddenly calmer, he sat down. "We are going to go over everything in detail, from the beginning. Answer my questions exactly."

He motioned to the clerk to begin to take notes. He interrogated me and, when each sentence was just right, he dictated it to the clerk, objectively, without seeking to involve me more deeply.

For more than an hour we meticulously retraced, according to my doctored version, my schedule for the day of December 24. Voituriez said nothing about the pistol and seemed to know nothing about Kalfort and Leplan, except for the "atmosphere of assassination that prevailed at the Coq Hardi." The Mobile Guards at the Summer Palace had not even mentioned that, after Bonnier got out, the Peugeot went toward Algiers and not toward Hydra.

In spite of their convictions, the Summer Palace people had no proof. They must have thought that the interrogation would easily supply it. How could the inquiry have been conducted so badly? Giraud must have kept quiet about his conversation with Henri d'Astier on December 25 ("Don't worry, I will do nothing for the moment"). Or else they preferred not to take it into consideration.

Voituriez stood up and walked around the room. His tone was more amenable. As if he were speaking to himself, he resumed. "During these last few days we have watched you go about, Henri d'Astier, Cordier, and you. We were persuaded that you would commit the mistake that would be your undoing — try to flee, some other reckless undertaking, a desperate action — and you did nothing. You opposed us only with your inertia."

I felt that he was a little distracted, but suddenly he turned to me.

"You played an active part in the American landing?"

"I had that honor."

"You are accustomed to clandestine operations. Then why did you put Bonnier de la Chapelle in your car in front of everyone?"

He could not believe that we had been, by some unspoken agreement, taking no precautions whatever. I stared at him to make him understand that his trick was getting nowhere.

He tried to find something else: "I am convinced that, above you, other people played a less incidental role. We know that you were often at the home of Henri d'Astier. How did you make his acquaintance?"

"He was my boss before the landing. He still is my boss."

"And Abbé Cordier?"

"I know Cordier as a member of the Resistance, not as a priest."

"And what else?"

"He is a friend, a companion in the struggle."

"Did you see the Count of Paris?"

"No."

"Did you ever have the impression that these powerful men were taking advantage of their influence to make use of you?

"No, never."

"Henri d'Astier has some very pretty daughters."

"Yes."

"Well then, perhaps I am not telling you anything new when I say that Henri d'Astier, who needed men for his work, was not sorry that his daughters' charm was attracting young men to his home, like Bonnier de la Chapelle, for example."

"What you're saying is infamous! You know nothing about his family. You cannot understand."

Voituriez planted himself in front of me.

"I asked you this question to see your reaction. So, if you wish, out of all that we will just keep my question, 'What do you think of Monsieur d'Astier?' and your answer, 'I like Monsieur d'Astier very much.'"

I signified that I would accept this, and the clerk wrote it down.

Voituriez opened a door opposite me, disappeared for a moment, and came back with a colonel: of medium height, looking like a clever

Cossack, it was surely Colonel Laroubine. He approached me without any hostility. In a conversational tone, he asked me what I knew about the fusillade in the Boulevard Baudin. I answered that at that moment, I was in the hall of police headquarters, that I rushed out on hearing the shots, but that when I reached the street it was over. He left after giving a sign of assent to Voituriez.

"Well, if anyone had told me when you entered here that you would come out free, I wouldn't have believed it," Voituriez said. "Naturally the inquiry is not finished, but you're free. You can leave as soon as you sign here."

He handed me the sheets of paper that the clerk had just given him. There were four pages. The interrogation had lasted more than three hours. I signed without reading them.

Voituriez opened the door and ordered the officers of the Mobile Guard to let me go. Dominique had waited for me in the corridor; now he left quickly to announce the news to Loffredo, while I went to the Rue Michelet. In front of the Lafferrière I ran into some comrades of the Free Corps. They had been certain that I was destined for the firing squad. We had a quick drink together, but I was in a hurry to get to the Rue La Fayette to parry the next blow that was surely being prepared.

Madame d'Astier and her daughters were happy and surprised to see me. I told my story rapidly and asked Marie-Béatrice and Arlette to go tell Jean-Bernard at the Maillot Hospital. Beyond any doubt, he was going to be interrogated in the coming hours in spite of his condition. It was absolutely necessary that his testimony should coincide with mine.

The next morning I stopped by La Robertsau, where Van Hecke was relieved to see me. "I was worried. Henri entrusted you to me. It's a good sign that they let you go."

Toward eleven I arrived at the Rue La Fayette. Madame d'Astier had gone to the military prison with some provisions which she was going to try to have delivered to her husband and Cordier. Marie-Béatrice and Arlette were just back from the hospital, where they had been that morning. Jean-Bernard had told them that last evening, a few minutes after their departure, the policemen had arrived. They interrogated him at length, until finally he was so weak that the doctors came and asked the policemen to leave.

What had we won? A hand? A round? None of us made any comments but, in silence, we nourished wild hopes of not being defeated by these people.

On the next morning, as I was going up the Boulevard Saint-Saëns, I was again arrested and taken to the DST. They shut me up in the little room with the painted glass panes, and a few minutes later Loffredo came in. He did not know what I was doing there. I briefly explained my system of defense.

"I've seen Voituriez," he told me. "I know about it. That may work: you made a strong impression on him. I don't know whether he believed you, but now it would be very difficult for him to send you to the firing squad."

Since the day before, new people had been assigned to the DST, doubtless to supervise what was going on. At about one in the afternoon Dominique reported that Roger Rosfelder had been brought back from Bordj-bou-Arréridj. He was in another room, and we could not see each other. I realized that Roger and I had not talked about coordinating our replies in case of an interrogation. We hadn't even broached the subject. After Bonnier's death it would not have seemed right. In any case, how could we have imagined that the inquiry would be conducted so badly?

The door opened again, and Loffredo entered the room cautiously. "It's not working," he said in a low voice. "Your pal is not on track. If I report to Voituriez what he is saying, you're done for."

"You're interrogating him?"

"Yes, I have a commission of inquiry. Voituriez is waiting, but he wants to receive the report no later than an hour from now."

"You must bring Roger to me. I'll talk with him, and then you can start over."

"That was possible yesterday, but not now."

"What are the inspectors like who are there at the interrogation?"

"One is all right; the other is an imbecile."

"Okay, you'll tear the paper up and start over. You let Roger speak and you write down only what you want."

The idea pleased him. "I'll see."

A moment later he came back. "It's okay. I did it that way."

Two days later we were arrested again. This time at the DST Loffredo had a commissioner by the name of Galopin placed over him. The inspectors pretended to be busy and to be paying no attention. Loffredo, whom I could see seated at his desk, made a gesture to signify that he was powerless.

Galopin interrogated us. Rather tall, dark, with distinguished features and an intelligent manner, he seemed nervous. In a severe tone but without conviction he asked us a few unimportant questions. Quite visibly he, too, wanted to provide a cover-up, but he did not know whom to trust.

At about two o'clock I was taken to the Rue Cavaignac and was once more led into the interrogation room. Voituriez, standing in a theatrical pose, assumed the tone of someone who was suffering intensely from a frightful betrayal.

"The other day I believed you, yes, I believed you! Well, I was wrong — because you lied to me!"

He waited and scrutinized me. "Why did you hide from me the fact that Jacques Brunel was having lunch with you also at the Paris?"

I answered that every day several friends had lunch at the Paris. I had attached no importance to the fact that Jacques Brunel might have been there that day. Moreover, the question had not been asked.

Walking back and forth in the room according to his custom, he let a little time go by; then he said, "Very good. That is all I wanted to know."

They took me back to the DST, and at six o'clock Galopin announced that we were free.

In the following days no one bothered us. On the contrary, Roger received permission to return to his camp at Bordj-bou-Arréridj. Why were Jean-Bernard, Roger, and I at liberty? What did Giraud want? What did Bergeret want? To shoot us? Just a few days earlier, that had been possible, especially if our role had been known to the man in the street. People would have wanted to show themselves to be without pity for anyone who, in wartime, attacked those in authority. But the inquiry had been conducted in the utmost secrecy and, in Algiers, the man in the street was not aware of any of it. At the Summer Palace the members of the junta therefore had a free hand, and they probably preferred not to raise the chaste veil that covered many plots in their harem. If they had wanted the truth to come out, they would not have kept Garidacci in solitary confinement.

Why would Voituriez have asked the question about Jacques Brunel, if not just to assure himself that I had seen nothing, heard nothing, and understood nothing at the luncheon at the Paris on December 24? If we had constituted a danger, or a risk that the affair might be exposed, we would unquestionably have joined Henri d'Astier, Cordier, Gilbert Sabatier, and Garidacci in solitary confinement at the military prison in the Pélissier barracks. Finally, it seemed that Laroubine and Voituriez had at last become convinced that, even if we knew more than our interrogations had led them to believe, we would not talk.

Furthermore, the Allied news correspondents, who were not held back by censorship, had taken the matter in hand. In the dispatches to London and New York and in the course of conversations in the drawing rooms of the Hôtel Aletti or the Hôtel Saint-Georges, they were severely criticizing the way the members of the Resistance were being treated in Algiers. It was likely that Giraud, Bergeret, Laroubine, and Voituriez preferred not to go ahead with new arrests. Perhaps, too, Giraud hesitated to burn his bridges, hoping to open negotiations with de Gaulle, who he must realize was now in the process of preparing his rise to power in Algiers.

I often had lunch at the Rue La Fayette. Winter had come, and it was cold in the unheated apartment. Sometimes Madame d'Astier put a little heating alcohol in a dish and lighted it. The little blue flame would warm our hearts. Our morale was good because it was out the question for any of us to make the slightest allusion to our adversity; but within us lived a great sadness. Pillafort and Bonnier were dead. The present and the future were a desert, nothing but the immense weight of memory interrupted by daily concerns.

Henri d'Astier and Cordier were held in the military prison. Jean-Bernard was very sick, drugged by the quinine necessary to check the violence of his attacks. Into this struggle we had thrown all of our strength, we realized, while little by little the tide receded.

Only once did Marie-Béatrice ask me what I thought about it all.

"Nothing at all."

February 1943. Our comrades who had been arrested on the night of December 29, then detained at Laghoust in the Algerian south, had been released. Jean-Bertrand was better. He was regaining strength, but his convalescence would be long.

One afternoon I was at the Elysée-Couturier talking with Guy Cohen. He informed me that Bernard Karsenty and Morali Daninos had arrived in London on January 8 with briefcases stuffed with documents and all our reports on the events here. They had been so active that the English had exerted pressure on the authorities to get Algiers to cease its repressive actions against the Resistance. A Jewish friend, David Zagha, was able to send a message to the Grand Rabbi of London, who intervened in his turn with the Grand Rabbi of New York. Telegrams of protest were flooding Murphy's desk. For several weeks the London and New York press had been denouncing the situation in Algiers. The press condemned the errors and the moral mistakes of Roosevelt, Murphy, and Eisenhower, criticizing them for having brought about here the opposite of what was to be expected of the ideals that inspired wartime America: the liberation of the occupied nations, the destruction of Naziism, the restoration of freedom. The American generals now said they were tired of the Vichyite conservatism that they themselves had left in place. Murphy had to distance himself from the Noguès and Bergeret clan and intervene in our favor. He was beginning to understand that we were not necessarily doomed to disappear.

It was on the orders of the Allied high command that our friends had been liberated. For reasons that were personal for each one of them, Giraud and Bergeret would keep Henri d'Astier and Cordier in prison as long as they could, but they were no longer pressing for inquiries. With the exception of Laroubine, Voituriez, and the clerk, who put it together in the utmost secrecy, Giraud was the only one to know of the dossier, and he refused to communicate it to anyone whatever. Laroubine, meanwhile promoted to the rank of general, had been summoned to the Summer Palace, where Giraud, who had already refused him permission to proceed against Alfred Pose and Marc Jacquet, declared that circumstances required that the affair be hushed up. He ordered him to classify it.

I asked Guy Cohen how he could explain that Roosevelt and Murphy were protecting us while continuing to break the Giraud-Murphy agreements and keeping those of Darlan and Clark.

"You know, Mario," he responded in his precise manner, "there are several currents in these Americans. They are impulsive and sentimental like big children, and that's where we are misled, because, at the same time, their minds and reflexes are very practical. So, on the one hand they want very much to have a clear conscience, but on the other hand they look after their own interests. Just by playing that game they have trapped themselves. They'll end up by installing de Gaulle, whom they don't want, whereas they thought they had maneuvered skillfully to get rid of him. And we will be out of favor in this adventure. Giraud has understood nothing. De Gaulle will remember very well that we did not act in his service alone. Who else has any interest in recognizing what we have done? You'll see, my dear Mario, that, whatever be our virtues, at the banquet of glory we will have to be satisfied with the crumbs."

For three months Algeria had been free, but the men of Vichy still ruled. On the high plateaus of the southern Atlas, the gates of the concentration camps of Bossuet, Méchéria, Boghar, Berrouaghia, Djarft, Adjerat M'Ghil were still shut. Political deportees suffered and died as they had done before November 8. In Algiers the pro-Nazi factions had not surrendered their arms, while a few little gold Crosses of Lorraine appeared on the lapels of mysterious and busy men who acted like bishops in civilian clothes, clutching their portfolios of future secretaries of state.

Daridan, Germain Libine, Marcel Fellus, Roger Rosfelder, and I had succeeded in joining the French forces. De Gaulle was in Algiers, now the capital of wartime France, as the leader of the provisional government; on his arrival all political detainees were set free. Gilbert Sabatier was released after six months in solitary confinement. Garidacci had been let out two months earlier.

The Darlan-Clark accords were annulled. Alfred Pillafort and Jean Dreyfus were posthumously named Compagnons de la Libération. The trial for the rehabilitation of Fernand Bonnier de la Chapelle was in progress. Henri d'Astier de la Vigerie and Pierre-Marie Cordier were released.

General de Gaulle put in place a Consultative Assembly and declared, "Any artificial creation of power besides mine will not be tolerated." Those who had opposed the regime were summoned. Bergeret was arrested and accused of arbitrary arrests and a royalist plot. Noguès fled to Portugal. The other Vichy leaders were in prison, with the exception of General Juin, whose dossier, "for reasons of state," was classified.

General Giraud, evicted from his last command, asked for asylum in England, but that appeal remained unanswered. Put under house arrest in a villa at Mostaganem, he was wounded by a shot fired under mysterious circumstances. A bullet went through his jaw.

Major Henri d'Astier de la Vigerie resigned from his position as a member of the Consultative Assembly and took command of the Special Detachment of the First Commando Group. Madame d'Astier, Marie-Béatrice, and Arlette joined the ambulance corps. Jean-Bernard d'Astier joined the First Commando Group.

Lieutenant Pierre-Marie Cordier was sent to the Italian front. His commanding officer, Captain Cadol, revealed to him that he had secretly received an order to take advantage of an enemy engagement to shoot him down.

De Gaulle alone held power. In 1941 he had gotten rid of Admiral Muselier, chief of the Free French naval forces and more popular than de Gaulle, by letting him be denounced to Churchill for complicity with Vichy, something that he knew to be false. In 1942 he had rid himself of the Count of Paris by putting him under the moral obligation to strike down Darlan, an obstacle that blocked his road to Algiers. He was neither a negotiator, nor an arbiter, nor a conciliator, nor a clan leader. He divided and crushed to assure his hegemony, and he considered France to be his legitimate possession. No one could tell whether he would reconstruct it to conform with his ethic or destroy it in pursuing his mythical goals. In Algiers, where personal ambition and political intrigue were running rampant while elsewhere a war was going on, de Gaulle was omnipotent. The process of his rise to power in metropolitan France was already under way.

On a night in the summer of 1944, I was in an American B-24 Liberator, which was going to parachute me into the Epinal region. Four hours earlier we had taken off from London. Now we were getting close. Under my jump suit I was wearing civilian clothes. Near me a red light blinked, indicating that the drop zone had been located by the navigator. The green light went on; the dispatcher shouted, "Go!" and I jumped. The dark mass of the great plane roared off in the night; the red rockets of the Wehrmacht rose from somewhere nearby into the sky to signal the alert. With my Colt in one pocket, my capsule of cyanide in another, as the odor of the soil of the Vosges came to greet me, I felt fine; within me there was nothing but peace.

Admiral François Darlan in 1939.

Admiral François Darlan and General Henri Giraud at the Admiralty.
Courtesy of ECPA — Etablissement Cinématographique et Photographique de l'Armée

Mont-Hydra, the Faivre family's villa.

Lieutenant Alfred Pillafort in Morocco during the Riff war, 1925.

Captain Alfred Pillafort a few days before the American landing.

Madame d'Astier de la Vigerie in 1942.

Lieutenant Pierre-Marie Cordier ("the abbé"), who planned the assassination.

The Summer Palace, where Darlan was assassinated.

A very fine view of the photogenic Palais d'été where Darlan was assassinated.
Photo Roger-Viollet Documentation Photographique, Paris, France

Fernand Bonnier de la Chapelle in Algiers, 1942.

General Henri Giraud decorating Henri d'Astier de la Vigerie on the first anniversary of the Algiers landing. D'Astier had just been released after nine months in prison.

Major Henri d'Astier de la Vigerie on the eve of the Allied landings in southern France in 1944.

Mario Faivre at the end of 1944, after his Operation Sussex mission in Alsace.

Below: Mario Faivre on the Austrian front in May 1945.

An excellent view of the Admiralty (the picture is called simply "The Waterfront in a Storm").
Photo Roger-Viollet Documentation Photographique, Paris, France.

The old port of Algiers where American commandos landed (and were captured).
Photo Roger-Viollet Documentation Photographique, Paris, France.

Postscript

by Douglas W. Alden

*O*N THIS BOOK Mario Faivre does not tell us how he came to be parachuting into France in 1944. That information can be pieced together from brief accounts in two of his subsequent books. In *Le Chemin du Palais d'été*, published in 1982, he informs us that he was put in command of several tanks when Van Hecke's Chantiers de la Jeunesse became the 7ᵉ régiment des Chasseurs d'Afrique, equipped with 36 tanks furnished by the Americans. Once, when the regiment was on maneuvers in the southern Atlas, it had to draw aside to let another convoy pass. This convoy was transporting the skeleton-like survivors who had been liberated from the Boghar concentration camp. Mario was so disgusted by the indifference of his fellow soldiers that he asked Colonel Van Hecke for permission to join the Free French: he did not feel at home in the regular French army. He was welcomed by the Free French, who sent him to Tunisia.

In his *Notes à propos de 1944*, published in 1994, Mario tells us what happened next. The Free French assigned him to a tank company in Syria (recently taken over by the Free French, aided by the

English) and sent him to the Syrian frontier with Turkey. Next, he was shipped back to Algiers, where he was attached to de Gaulle's office at the Villa des Glycines. Then he joined the BCRA, the French equivalent of the American OSS, which was already preparing the joint Sussex operation. Mario does not say when he was parachuted into France. My memory is not as good as his, but it must have been somewhat after D-Day, since he was sent far into the interior to prepare for the advance of the American 7th Army. The first date he gives is September 5, when the Germans burned the village of Rehaincourt and deported its inhabitants in reprisal for a *maquis* (French underground) attack.

As in all our missions, Mario was part of a team of two, an observer and a radio operator, although training and functions were interchangeable. From the very beginning they worked closely with the local *maquis*, part of the FFI (*Forces Françaises de l'Intérieur*) and, for all intents and purposes, became members of it, participating finally in battles against the Germans. In due course, their *maquis* became a combat group in the French Division Leclerc attached to the 7th Army. With the Germans pushed back or surrounded, Mario and his teammate, Jean Berton, tried to volunteer for the American army but were refused because members of the *maquis* had to report to the French army. Thus Mario found himself at the DGER, formerly the BCRA, in Paris, where he made a brief report for the OSS archives.

In Paris he met up with Major Henri d'Astier de la Vigerie, whose commando unit had fought its way north from Saint Tropez on the Mediterranean and was then taking part in the siege of Belfort. Mario joined this unit and then was assigned to the 5th Armored Division of the French army. At the Battle of Königsbach he was commended for taking command of his unit when the commanding officer was seriously wounded. At Waldrenach his bravery was again commended. In all, he received four Croix de Guerre citations, and in 1946 he received the decoration of Chevalier de la Légion d'Honneur.

For the American reader in particular, Mario's *We Killed Darlan* raises many questions. I will try to answer them.

Why did the Americans choose Darlan? In his *Calculated Risk*, General Clark says that he and General Eisenhower had as a major objective to bring the French army in North Africa over to the American side, and that Darlan's name entered into the discussions. Clark writes, commenting on a long cable from Murphy before the Cherchell meeting, that Murphy "wanted to know, first, were we willing to cooperate with Darlan . . . in an effort to secure his cooperation with Giraud." In Professor Arthur Layton Funk's remarkable study, *The Politics of Torch*, we get further elucidation of this surprising information. The idea that Darlan was willing to cooperate, according to Funk, goes back to Darlan's statement to Leahy on August 1, 1941: "When you have 300 tanks, 600 planes, and 500,000 men to bring to Marseilles, let me know. Then we shall welcome you." Funk continues, "Darlan did not intend this statement as sarcastic or humorous; he meant it very much in earnest and he repeated it many times to American representatives."

Professor Funk has called to my attention what he considers to be an excellent book in French entitled *Darlan*, published by Hervé Coutau-Bégarie and Claude Huan in 1989. These authors insist that Darlan's remark was inadvertent and was made in a moment of vexation when Leahy was reproaching Darlan for collaborating so closely with the Germans. Be that as it may, the fact remains that this remark gave birth to an American mystique: if 500,000 men were mentioned, there would be cooperation.

It is a fact that, when he began to doubt the invulnerability of Germany, Darlan directed his son Alain and Admiral Raymond Fenard to set up a line of communication with the Americans by inviting Murphy to dinner, which they did on April 11, 1942. Darlan's message indicated that he might eventually want to discuss an invasion of southern France. Funk comments, "The statement did not suggest that Darlan was ready to conspire with the United States; it simply conveyed a plea that if Washington had in mind the long-range interests of France it would not do anything so stupid that North Africa and southern France would be occupied or the fleet would be jeopardized."

In September Colonel Jean Chrétien, chief of army intelligence in North Africa, learned through his spy Bègue (whose life Pillafort and Mario spared) that the Americans were planning to invade North Africa before November 15, and Chrétien went to Vichy to warn Darlan. Darlan authorized him to contact the Americans; Murphy, accompanied by Saint-Hardouin and d'Astier de la Vigerie, met with Chrétien and promised the legendary 500,000 men without saying when. Darlan persisted in believing that an American invasion was logistically impossible before spring 1943.

In another conference with Major André Dorange, Juin's aide (who plays an important role in Mario's narrative), Murphy was told that Juin would defend North Africa against all comers, to which Murphy replied, "We will not set foot on French territory without an invitation." On October 28, after a tour of the defenses of North Africa, Darlan studied Dorange's report to Juin and was aware of Murphy's statement about the invitation.

If we follow Professor Funk's account of what happened at Juin's residence on the night of the landings, we discover that Mario was misinformed. Juin and Darlan were not Murphy's prisoners. When Giraud failed to arrive, Murphy, with the consent of the Group of Five (actually four, because Van Hecke, uninformed about the timing of the invasion, was away on official business), went immediately to confer with General Juin, undoubtedly hoping that Juin himself would consent to fill the gap caused by Giraud's absence. He first sent Knight to get Chrétien, and then all three went to Juin's villa. Juin said, "I would be with you," but that any order he gave would be countermanded by Darlan, who happened to be in Algiers again incognito, to visit Alain, hospitalized by polio. Hoping that Darlan likewise would be cooperative, Murphy asked that he be summoned.

Meanwhile, Lieutenant Pauphilet had arrived with only six men; the 60 whom he had expected had not appeared at the rendezvous. With orders from General Mast, he took command of the guard but did not dare dismiss it since he had so few men. He never went inside the villa and never arrested anyone. Things went on for a while as though the normal guard were in place, and Admiral Darlan, accompanied by Vice Consul Kenneth Pendar, passed in without noticing anything. When Darlan learned why he had been summoned, he became furious because of Murphy's promise not to violate French territory. He also thought that he was being led into a trap: that the Americans could not have sufficient troops and that the invasion of Algiers was only another Dakar or another Dieppe. After much argument, he finally said that he must consult Vichy; Murphy agreed that he could prepare a message to be hand-delivered to the Admiralty for transmission to Pétain. In this message Darlan reported what was happening and said he would obey any order from Pétain. This, at least, gave Pétain the opportunity to rescind the previous order to resist any attack on North Africa. Mario was correct in saying that the first message was never sent; instead of taking it to the Admiralty, Pendar made a detour by way of 26 Rue Michelet, where it was confiscated. Mario says, however, that a second message did get through. In his book, Professor Funk does not mention this second message. He tells me now that there was a second message but that he did not know about it when he wrote his book.

Discussions with Darlan ended abruptly when Major Dorange arrived with a detachment of Mobile Guards commanded by Colonel Zwilling, who captured Pauphilet and his men, as well as Murphy and Pendar. Believing they were about to be shot, Murphy and Pendar were rescued by Juin, who held them at his villa. According to Funk, Juin ordered his troops to maintain "elastic contact without aggressivity." (I have found the same statement in an official publication of the French navy, *Les Débarquements alliés en Afrique du Nord*.) Finally realizing that he was not facing another Dieppe but an enemy with superior power, Darlan sent for Murphy and asked him to broker a cease-fire with General Charles W. Ryder, as Clark had not yet arrived.

By this time Murphy had lost all interest in Giraud. When Giraud finally did arrive, Murphy was at Blida airfield, hoping to meet Clark, who was delayed by weather. Murphy brushed Giraud aside and, thinking he was at the wrong airfield, rushed off to Maison Blanche. Clark, in his memoirs, wrote, "I had talked briefly to Giraud and found that he had quickly discovered that his relations with the French officers in North Africa were none too good. He decided to await developments and instead of trying to seize the leadership, he practically went underground, moving in with a French family in an obscure neighborhood after letting us know where to find him." The "French family" was Lemaigre-Dubreuil, and the residence was the Villa Mahieddine, owned by the Faivres.

With no Giraud, Clark was in difficulty: the cease-fire applied only to Algiers, and things were going badly in Casablanca and Oran. Earlier, Murphy had stopped at Casablanca in the expectation that Noguès would react favorably to the idea of an American invasion. Noguès invited Murphy to dinner but declared that he would obey Pétain's orders and would resist the Americans "with all of the firepower that I possess."

In contrast to Algiers, the battles at Casablanca, Oran, and elsewhere resulted in severe losses on both sides. Allied casualties were 534 dead, 937 wounded, 63 missing, and 44 planes shot down. French losses: 1,100 dead, 1,492 wounded, and 472 planes shot down. Counting losses at Mers-el-Kébir, France had now sacrificed half of its entire fleet.

In a chapter called "The Darlan Deal," Clark tells how he argued interminably with Darlan and the assembled French officers, who disagreed among themselves until he thumped on the table and shouted. His first task was to coerce Darlan into extending the cease-fire. At one point he even had to call in troops and threaten Darlan with arrest. At first Darlan was very dejected and refused to act without consulting Vichy. Coutau-Bégarie and Huan explain his motivation as loyalty to Pétain and fear that a false move would precipitate the German occupation of the Free Zone and the loss of the Toulon fleet. After the Germans did occupy the Free Zone, Darlan began to cooperate with Clark and even ordered the fleet at Toulon to move to Dakar. As Mario told us, Admiral Laborde followed the original order and scuttled the fleet instead. Noguès, who had now surrendered, came to Algiers from Morocco, and other generals and admirals fell into line. Clark had finally achieved his objective, an obedient French army soon fighting beside the Allies in Tunisia.

By not firing Darlan, Clark also had a competent civil administrator. Among Darlan's papers was even a draft for a future constitution modeled on that of the United States. Darlan complained to a friend that he was being treated as a small boy rather than a five-star admiral, and in his memoirs Clark admits that, in private, he always referred to Darlan as "the little fellow." Nevertheless he was surprised when a young university student "yelled some unintelligible phrase while firing four shots point blank at the admiral." He adds, "I don't know what this meant politically. I issued immediate orders alerting all our troops. . . ." He finally calls Darlan's death "an act of Providence. . . . His removal from the scene was like the lancing of a troublesome boil." He did not seem to be aware that the Resistance existed or that anything bordering on promises to them had been made at Cherchell.

Why did Giraud fail to come on time? The answer, of course, is that he obstinately insisted on commanding Operation Torch. This was not altogether Murphy's fault. Among Giraud's papers was a message copied in his own handwriting that said that if he joined the North African invasion he would have supreme command, something that must have seemed reasonable to him since he was a seasoned general, whereas the Americans had never been in combat, and since American troops had been under Marshal Ferdinand Foch in World War I. Professor Funk asserts that there is no proof that this was an authentic American message. At Gibraltar, Giraud startled Eisenhower and Clark by insisting that he had been promised supreme command of the operation. They argued politely with him for three hours and then resumed the next day. There was a complete stalemate, while the landings themselves went forward. Clark thinks Giraud was stalling to assess the outcome of the landings. After the cease-fire in Algiers was in effect, he finally left Gibraltar and expected to land at Blida with bands blaring and with full support of the French army.

What happened next is summarized by Mario in his later book, *Le Chemin du Palais d'été*, on the basis of the memoirs of General Mast, *Alger, 8 novembre 1942, Histoire d'une rébellion* (1969). While Clark was still arguing with Darlan on November 10, Major Dorange called upon Giraud in the morning with the intention of demoralizing him by convincing him that the French army would never obey a "dissident general." General Mast, General de Monsabert, Lemaigre-Dubreuil, Henri d'Astier, Captain Beaufre, and others were trying to restore Giraud's morale when Clark and Murphy arrived. In a meeting witnessed by the French generals, Clark told Giraud that Darlan had ordered a cease-fire for all Algeria and was in effect a prisoner, and that the Allies needed him, Giraud, to take charge of the French government and to lead the French army against the Germans in Tunisia. Giraud still obstinately insisted on being the supreme commander. Clark and Murphy left abruptly, and we know the rest: Clark had no recourse but to deal with Darlan to get the support of the French army. At this juncture Mario makes his most pro-American remark: "Both [Clark and Murphy] had loyally kept the American promises and offered our leader the chance to take power."

Of course, Clark did not give up entirely on Giraud. During his later consultations with Darlan, Clark insisted that Giraud and Mast be present, even though the other French officers turned their backs on them. In the long run, Clark's high-handed methods were so successful that he did succeed in getting Darlan and his officers to appoint Giraud as the supreme French commander, even above Juin.

Why did the Americans fail to support the Resistance? First, there is the matter of the weapons that were not delivered. Clark says that he promised Mast "delivery of two thousand small arms with ammunition by submarine at the earliest practicable date." The weapons were in fact scheduled to arrive, but Professor Aboulker went to the wrong beach, according to Coutau-Bégarie and Huan, quoting the French edition of Murphy's memoirs.

Then there is the more important matter of the commandos who never arrived, as promised, to relieve the Resistance forces. Mario gives the impression that the main battle was raging in the port. The basic American strategy in North Africa was first to encircle the cities. Tank-landing craft (LST's) had not been invented, so landing in the dark with traditional small boats created enormous confusion. Until dawn the Allied troops went undetected; then some units came under the guns of Cape Matifou. At the fort of Sidi Ferruch British commandos met no resistance because General Mast had taken command, and after taking the two airports without difficulty they were preparing to bombard Fort l'Empereur on the edge of the city when Darlan decided to give up at six in the evening.

At one point Mario says, "The Allied warships which tried to penetrate into the harbor received serious damage." It is quite true that, contrary to the usual strategy, two British destroyers did try to land American commandos, who might have relieved the Resistance. Both ships were badly damaged and had to withdraw. The commandos who had landed were marooned, and they surrendered after 15 of them had been killed. As for Mario's "three-stack troopship" breaking through the barrier, there is no mention of it in other accounts, including the French navy's report.

The Resistance did indeed serve the purpose of disorganizing the French army and, as Funk says, invented a new kind of guerrilla warfare.

Were the Cherchell accords flouted? There is no doubt that the Americans deceived the French; General Clark admits it. He says that he misled the French by claiming that he would provide the proverbial 500,000 men, whereas he really had, he asserted, only 120,000 American and British troops. Even that figure was not altogether accurate, according to an article by Christine Levisse-Touzé, author of an unpublished doctoral dissertation on the Algiers landings. She states that Clark had only 106,500 men, of whom 23,000 were British. Of the 33,000 men who landed in Algiers, only 10,000 were American. Clark's refusal to disclose the date of the landings might also fall into the category of deceit.

Mario felt that the Resistance had been betrayed by the failure of the Americans to live up to the "Giraud-Clark accords." Murphy took with him to Cherchell two documents; one was the economic accord, for which he expected Washington's approval because it was based on the earlier agreement with Weygand; the other was the draft of a letter to Giraud. Mario seemed to think that these documents were nearly definitive because they had been drawn up by Murphy as the special representative of President Roosevelt, and that, in any event, they were fully approved at Cherchell. That was not the case. Murphy knew that any document emanating from the Cherchell meeting would have to be approved by Eisenhower and ultimately by Washington.

Although Clark says nothing about these documents in his memoirs and records his surprise at Giraud's insistence on supreme command at Gibraltar, Professor Funk's account of the meeting, based on research and interviews with some of the participants, shows that Clark participated in these discussions and was well aware of all of the ramifications. The most important issue was precisely whether Giraud should command the entire operation. Murphy's draft letter to Giraud said originally, "The general direction of operations would be exercised by you." At Cherchell this text was modified to read, "While French forces are being equipped and organized the command machinery can be perfected so as to permit French assumption of the supreme command at the appropriate time." The letter also contained a guarantee of the territorial integrity of France and its Empire. Giraud never received such a letter. All he got was a summary of the meeting, somewhat incomplete and prepared in haste by Rigault. From a memorandum of the Joint Chiefs of Staff of January 7, 1943, it is clear that the guarantee of territorial integrity would not have been approved, for the memorandum quotes Roosevelt as saying, ". . . In doing this Mr. Murphy exceeded his authority."

The so-called Darlan-Clark agreements naming Darlan as high commissioner necessarily superseded the unapproved Cherchell agreements. Funk records the new document in his appendix. It deals primarily with the relations between the American and French forces; it specifies that the civil authorities will remain in place if they are not disloyal to the American army; and it establishes censorship. On the more positive side, it calls for an economic commission and for the liberation of political detainees (something that was never accomplished under either Darlan or Giraud).

What about the Count of Paris? Probably American readers are just as astonished as Mario was by this intrusion of the Orléans pretender into the muddled politics of North Africa. As Mario presents it, this will seem to the reader to be only a misguided attempt to find a leader by the Group of Five, who once imagined themselves as the nucleus of a new government for North Africa. Surely they were taking a great risk in supposing that they could successfully confront the American military authorities with a fait accompli. It seems strange that there was such wide support for the plan, even among the French officers as well as the Jews. In retrospect, the whole idea seems ludicrous, especially given the personality, or rather lack of personality, of the prince. Mario seems to be reluctant to meet him, and Henri d'Astier, royalist though he is at heart, discovers that the prince is "not as bad" as he had originally thought. Of course, Mario, as usual, is putting words in his mouth (a practice to which a professional historian with whom I have corresponded objects strenuously).

The assassination does not fit into such a simplified version of the events. Mario thinks of it as the collective act of the Resistance. To be sure, 50 hot-headed young men at Cape Matifou would have done the deed, but that does not signify unanimity in the Resistance or consent of the entire Group of Five. On a closer look, one person seems responsible, Henri d'Astier, who feels compelled, in spite of his better nature, to carry out the prince's order. Yet, after passing the order on to Cordier, he stands aloof from the whole procedure. This strange aloofness is never explained. On the other hand, Cordier did not act alone but received mysterious assistance from other quarters. If d'Astier and, presumably, the prince were opposed to de Gaulle, why did they obey? If we can believe Mario once more, d'Astier explained his motivation thus: "To refuse to execute this order was to confirm everything against which we have struggled, to cut us off from the Resistance in metropolitan France, in a word, to betray our cause."

What really happened, and why, have never been fully explained. Giraud and Bergeret, after arresting the Resistance leaders, ordered a reluctant Colonel Laroubine to make a thorough investigation on the presumption that de Gaulle was implicated. Laroubine passed the responsibility on to a subordinate from Casablanca, Major Voituriez, who many years later gave an extensive account of his experience in his *L'Affaire Darlan, l'instruction judiciaire* (1980). Voituriez knew nothing about what had happened and was given no information. He discovered that the file of Bonnier's trial contained only a page with Bonnier's signature, above which was a brief, possibly forged, statement. According to French law, there should have been a record of the interrogation before the trial; the clerk of the court-martial said that he was not allowed to make a record, and Voituriez could not get permission to interrogate the presiding judge. He then proceeded to question the prisoners, d'Astier, Cordier,

Achiary, and finally Garidacci. Achiary talked freely because, as a republican, he disapproved of the royalist machinations. Voituriez asked to have the Count of Paris brought in, but Giraud refused and sent the Count back to Morocco the next day. Next, Voituriez discovered that the leader of the plot was Pose, Giraud's finance minister, but Giraud refused to touch him because he was needed for negotiations with the Americans. Shortly after he had conferred with de Gaulle at Anfa, Giraud ordered Voituriez to "classify" the entire affair on the pretext that revelation of the details would make a bad impression on the Americans. Voituriez' files are not in the French archives.

In their *Darlan*, Coutau-Bégarie and Huan consider it plausible that de Gaulle gave the assassination order. Although mistrustful of Mario, in spite of frequent references to *Nous avons tué Darlan*, they agree essentially with him that the assassination eliminated simultaneously two of de Gaulle's rivals, the Count of Paris and Darlan. The two historians conclude, however, that it was all a far-reaching monarchist plot, that the Count's real goal was the throne of France.

It was Pose (the clown cavorting in General d'Astier's cloak and cap) who engineered the plan to bring the prince to Algiers as an idealistic leader, in the hope that, in a further step, he might become king. In 1982, in his *Le Chemin du Palais d'été*, after expressing indignation that the prince in his memoirs denied having any part in the assassination, Mario calls the assassination itself, without further comment, "an attempt to establish the dynasty."

According to Coutau-Bégarie and Huan, Henri d'Astier was not only a monarchist participating in a plot to enthrone the Count of Paris, but he was also a Gaullist agent and even offered to meet de Gaulle in Gibraltar to plan for the elimination of Darlan. After the assassination of Darlan, he allegedly was expecting to assassinate Jean Rigault because he knew too much. They quote Garidacci quoting Bonnier: "In the course of our conversations M. d'Astier showed me that the only solution for France to have a brilliant future was to return to the monarchy. . . . M. d'Astier led me to understand that I could one day become an ambassador. And then his daughters were nice. . . ." The two historians go on to claim that Bonnier's fiancée was really "Beatrice d'Astier de la Vigerie."

In the light of all that Mario said about d'Astier's character, the reader must find it difficult to believe all of this so-called evidence. In his *Qui a tué Darlan?*, published in 1992, Mario's friend Jean-Bernard d'Astier de la Vigerie attempts to refute such allegations. He denies that his father ever met Bonnier, but he does say further on that Bonnier was his own friend and came frequently to his home. Note that Mario says, "On several occasions [Bonnier] visited Henri d'Astier and Cordier." As for the assertion that "Béatrice" was the fiancée, Jean-Bernard says merely that her name was "Marie-Béatrice," as though this information sufficed to confound our two historians. He defends his father from the accusation of being a Gaullist spy, describing in detail his distinguished record in two world wars and asserting that, for unspecified reasons, de Gaulle ordered the prefect of Corsica to arrest his father when d'Astier's commando unit docked there in 1944 on its way to southern France. A large part of Jean-Bernard's book is devoted to a narrative, largely duplicating Mario's, of the details of the assassination. Like Mario, he insists that the order to assassinate came from de Gaulle by way of his Uncle François.

Who was Fernand Bonnier de la Chapelle? A coincidence has put me in touch with still another variant of the fiancée story. At a dinner in the mountains near Charlottesville, Virginia, to make conversation with a Belgian lady beside me, I began to talk about Mario's book. Our hostess, Dr. Françoise Attinger, exclaimed in French, "I know who assassinated Darlan. It was Fernand Bonnier de la Chapelle. I knew him in Paris. His fiancée became our daughter's godmother." Pursuing the matter further with Françoise, I have learned that she knew Bonnier well during that period, not only because his fiancée was her close friend but also because the young man was frequently at the home of his Uncle Gaston, who lived in the next building. She recalls that Fernand was a fervent Gaullist. She recalls also that, in the summer of 1943, having special permission to cross the line of demarcation, she was in her family's house in Dordogne with the fiancée and some other friends when they heard for the first time on the radio that Darlan's assassin was Bonnier de la Chapelle. At the time of the assassination, General Bergeret had announced officially that the assassin was a German agent sent to punish Darlan for collaborating with the Americans. So far this much was certain: at the time of the assassination, two young ladies thought that Bonnier de la Chapelle would marry them.

Seeking more information about Fernand Bonnier de la Chapelle, at Françoise's suggestion I wrote to Gaston Bonnier de la Chapelle, now 94, still living in Paris at the same address. He responded by sending me a

copy of a poignant appeal, undated, from Eugène Bonnier de la Chapelle
to rehabilitate his son. The governor general in Algiers replied sympathet-
ically on November 15, 1943, and then passed the appeal on to Giraud,
who responded perfunctorily; no action was taken for two years. After his
rehabilitation in 1945, Fernand Bonnier was decorated posthumously in
1953 with the Médaille Militaire, the Croix de Guerre avec Palme, and the
Médaille de la Résistance.

From material in the appeal, and from an article by the historian Alain
Decaux in *Histoire Magazine* for December 1980, which Mario sent me, I
can now construct a biography of the younger Fernand Bonnier de la
Chapelle. When his parents were divorced in Algiers, Fernand was
entrusted to his Uncle Fernand in Paris, where he attended several private
schools. Because he was the leader of an anti-German student group and
was on the Germans' black list, at the urging of his uncle he escaped to
Marseilles, in the vain hope of escaping to London with Gaullist friends.
Next he went home to Algiers and, bored with studies at the *lycée*, enlisted
in the Air Force. He tried to steal an airplane at Blida in order to reach
Gibraltar, but when he was gassing up the plane in the dark he lit a candle
to see better. The subsequent explosion would have resulted in a court
martial and a firing squad if the colonel had not called in none other than
Achiary, who persuaded the colonel that Bonnier acted alone and was
really a patriot at heart. His only punishment was dismissal from the Air
Force. After a compulsory stint in the Chantiers de la Jeunesse, in June
1941 he passed the second half of his *baccalauréat*, started and then
dropped the study of law at the university, and on November 7, 1942, was
about to embark on the S.S. *El Biar*, to join his uncle Fernand and study
in Lyons when his friends told him that something momentous was about
to happen. He dumped his baggage in his father's front hall and joined the
Resistance.

Should Darlan have been assassinated? Without considering the eth-
ical issues, it is clear that the assassination accomplished nothing but put
all the good people in jail. Obviously there was no intention to bring back
Giraud, although that is what happened. Mario ended up just not giving a
damn. Henri d'Astier and Cordier, according the Mario, were afflicted
with remorse but not for Darlan's demise. A sad ending for the glorious
undertaking of the Algiers Resistance.

Voituriez told Mario that the assassination was a mistake because Darlan would not have lasted long. In an article, "Assassination Victim Un-mourned," in a periodical called *World War II*, Professor Funk makes the same argument. Because of criticism in the press, Roosevelt had announced that Darlan was only a "temporary expedient." In a letter to Roosevelt on November 21, Darlan wrote that he expected to be cast aside "like a crushed lemon."

How did de Gaulle come to power in Algeria? Mario leaves no doubt that in 1975, when he wrote his book, he was violently opposed to de Gaulle. Did he allow his feelings in 1975 to intrude on his feelings of 1940 because of his opposition, as a former *colon*, to de Gaulle's dismemberment of the Empire?

Washington's mistrust of de Gaulle increased at the time of Darlan's death because it was believed that there was some connection between that event and General d'Astier's visit. There was also tension between Roosevelt and Churchill regarding policy in North Africa. Churchill felt that American control of North Africa was too exclusive, and he was anxious to insert a British element in the person of de Gaulle, even if he was cantankerous. The January 14 Casablanca conference was intended to be a military consultation for the invasion of Sicily, but it also turned into a political event because Roosevelt brought along his protégé Giraud. Because of Giraud's presence, Churchill sent an urgent message to de Gaulle to come over. After difficult negotiations over subsequent months, de Gaulle finally arrived in Algiers on May 30, 1943, at the same time as Churchill and General Marshall.

In principle, de Gaulle and Giraud were to be cochairmen of a French Committee of National Liberation. Stamping in and out of meetings, de Gaulle finally secured complete political control but had to yield military command to Giraud. Until that time, two armies existed side by side: one was Giraud's ex-Vichy army; the other was the Free French army, which had been with Field Marshal Bernard Montgomery and had distinguished itself in Leclerc's epic campaign across the Libyan desert and in Koenig's courageous defense of the pass at Bir Hakeim against Rommel's entire army. Thousands were deserting from Giraud's forces to join the Free French. While Giraud was in Washington seeking supplies for his army, de Gaulle was winning over the support of the people of Algiers by public appearances. This was the beginning of Giraud's decline. He was gradually denied assignments and was finally put on the retired list in April 1944.

On August 26, 1943, Britain and the United States, with some reservations, recognized de Gaulle's government, and 37 other countries followed suit.

The Faivre family. In recent correspondence Mario has answered a number of questions. One was, How long had your family been in Algeria? On the maternal side, Charles Branthomme came to Algiers in 1831 and was the first mayor of the city. Another ancestor, General Pierre Germain, founded a "domain" by draining the marshes near Mitidja. Mario's mother's maiden name was Geneviève Germain. On the paternal side, grandmother Marie-Félicité Régnier's family came from Vésoul in 1848 to found the oldest "pioneer village," Vésoul-Bénain. Since there were no Régnier sons, two Faivre cousins were brought over from Franche-Comté shortly after 1870 to marry two Régnier daughters. Xavier-Jules Faivre, Mario's grandfather, was the mayor of Vésoul-Bénain before moving to Algiers.

In his narrative, Mario has already presented his father as a poet, a journalist, and the leading intellectual of Algiers. The September 1989 number of *L'Algérianiste*, a periodical published in Montpellier, was dedicated to Marcello-Fabri, whose real name was Marcel-Louis Faivre. On the cover is a painting of this elegant young man at 22, wearing a felt hat and sporting a "Newgate fringe" beard and a wisp of a mustache. At 17, he was already collaborating in periodicals; at 20, he published *Hallucinations*, his first volume of poetry. In Algiers he frequented a milieu of writers and painters, and in 1919, with his wife of four years, he moved to Paris, where he already knew several prominent writers, and founded a periodical, *La Revue de l'Epoque*. Mario was born in Paris. In 1925 the family moved back to Algiers and purchased Mont-Hydra, a magnificent Moorish-style villa surrounded by flowers and palm trees. Next, Faivre formed the Federation of Intellectual Workers of Algeria, bringing together all the intellectuals and artists of the city. Hoping to produce a fusion of Algerian and Parisian cultures, he moved to Paris again in 1937 and founded a periodical, *L'Age Nouveau*. His own works were now appearing under the imprint of a leading publishing house, the Mercure de France. In August 1939, as war was breaking out, the family returned to Mont-Hydra. Some of his works have recently appeared in special editions that include his poems, his paintings, and his melodious prose.

Another question was, Who was Denise? She appears first as one of the spectators in the Bois de Boulogne in Algiers during the bombardment; we learn that she is a refugee from Alsace. Later Mario goes to meet her at the girls' *lycée*; he notes that she is "blond and pretty" with blue eyes and a "charming nose." After the assassination, driving by in his Peugeot, Mario picks her up; she does not altogether approve of what has happened. Finally, just before his arrest, he says goodbye to her and she gives him a lock of her hair. These discreet interludes in such a somber story intrigued me. Here is Mario's answer: "In Alsace on October 25, 1945, I married Denise Winkler, whom I had known in Algiers where she and her parents had taken refuge after having lost all of their possessions in Alsace."

On December 7, 1945, Mario and his new wife returned to Algiers, Mario now released from the French army. His father died a few days after his return, and he and his brother Gérard, with a French government loan, rehabilitated the seven "domains" that his father had owned.

Algeria was no longer the idyllic country of prewar years. No sooner had de Gaulle left in 1944 than revolt broke out in the Kabyli region. The situation grew worse in the 1950s, when a major war between the entire French army and the FLN (Front de Libération Nationale) left 24,000 French and 150,000 Arabs dead. In France the political situation became so desperate that General de Gaulle, who had resigned in 1946, was brought back in 1958 to become prime minister while a new constitution was being drawn up. In the next election he became president, and in January 1959 he announced his new policy of "autodetermination" for Algeria: the Arabs and the French would have equal votes in determining the future government. While so-called "pacification" continued, along with major disturbances, autodetermination was approved as a policy by a 70-percent vote in 1961.

From May 1961 on, the French government and the FLN negotiated the terms of independence, including respect for the rights of the French in Algiers. On May 7, 1962, Algeria became independent. At Oran, 1,500 French were massacred. One source says that 700,000 French fled Algeria. I have not asked Mario when he and Denise left or under what circumstances, to avoid bringing up unpleasant memories. I know only that they lost all their possessions in Algeria.

They moved to Cannes, where they purchased a boatyard for yachts. Mario sold the boatyard in 1976 and was at last able to devote himself to music. His music is commercially available on cassettes, the latest one entitled *Musiques et arabesques.*

Included with the photocopies of various documents that Mario has sent me is a most unusual one. It is a petition signed (if they were literate, otherwise fingerprinted beside the name) by 78 employees of the domain of Kandoury-Attaba who, in 1963, are requesting the Algerian government to allow their *patron* (boss) to return because they need him. They express their gratitude for all that he has done for them, particularly for the buildings that he has constructed at his own expense: a dispensary with a nurse in residence and with free medicine; a school with lodging for teachers and uniforms for the children, even with prizes at the end of the school year; a mosque, which is the pride of the village; 100 houses, most with electricity and running water; finally a cinema with 350 seats. Mr. Faivre always paid good salaries and loaned money without interest to any employee in need. The petitioners "respectfully" entreat the government to assure "our boss that he runs no risk in Algeria."

Today, Mario says, the domains are in ruins and the employees are surviving on roots.

As this book goes to the printer, a new book has appeared, George E. Melton's *Darlan: Admiral and Statesman of France, 1881-1942*. Commendable for its objectivity and thorough documentation, it manifestly seeks to rehabilitate Darlan as a statesman acting to save France not only under the Vichy regime but also during his last 40 days in Algiers. For the reader of Mario Faivre's book, it will supply additional information on Darlan's relations with the English, on his earliest contacts with the Americans, and on his conduct in Algiers. Melton's version of the assassination follows closely the accounts of Mario Faivre and Voituriez and reaches the conclusion that either de Gaulle ordered the deed or that General d'Astier, to spare de Gaulle, acted in his name but on his own initiative, forcing the royalist plotters to eliminate by their own action de Gaulle's two rivals, Darlan and the Count of Paris.

I wish to thank Professor Emeritus Arthur Layton Funk of the University of Florida for his generous guidance and assistance in the early stages of my Introduction and Postscript, although he should in no way be held responsible for their final form. I am particularly beholden to Mario Faivre for additional information, documentation, and photographs, some of which he obtained from his friends, Madame Jean-Bernard d'Astier de la Vigerie and Jacques Poutet de Chazal. Mrs. Abigail Siddall, editor for Sunflower University Press, has done an incredible job putting into the past tense a narrative written in the present tense.

References

Aron, Robert. *Histoire de Vichy, 1940-1944*. Paris: Librairie Arthème Fayard, 1954.

Clark, Mark W. *Calculated Risk*. New York: Harper, 1950.

Coutau-Bégarie, Hervé, and Claude Huan. *Darlan*. Paris: Fayard, 1989.

_____. *Mers-el-Kébir: La rupture franco-britannique*. Paris: Economica, 1994.

Crémieux-Brilhac, Jean-Louis. *La France Libre: De l'appel du 18 juin à la Libération*. Paris: Gallimard, 1996.

d'Astier de la Vigerie, Jean-Bernard. *Qui a tué Darlan?* Versailles: Editions de l'Atlanthrope, 1992.

Faivre, Mario. *Le Chemin du Palais d'été: Alger 1942*. Paris: Regirex-France, 1982.

_____. *Notes à propos de 1944*. Cannes: Editions Santa Maria & Gazelle, 1994.

_____. *Nous avons tué Darlan: Alger 1942*. Paris: La Table Ronde, 1975.

Funk, Arthur Layton. *Charles de Gaulle: The Crucial Years, 1943-1944.* Norman: University of Oklahoma Press, 1959.

_____. *The Politics of Torch: The Allied Landings and the Algiers* Putsch, *1942.* Lawrence: The University of Kansas Press, 1979.

Laffont, Pierre. *Histoire de la France en Algérie.* Paris: Plon, 1980.

Melton, George E. *Darlan: Admiral and Statesman of France, 1881-1942.* Westport, CT: Praeger, 1998.

Index

by Lori L. Daniel